BACK TO ROUTINE

DEPRESSION, RELATIONSHIPS AND READJUSTMENT AFTER THE HOLIDAYS

DAVID SANDUA

INDEX

I. INTRODUCTION

The holiday season is often regarded as a joyous time for celebration, indulgence, and spending quality moments with loved ones. As the festivities wind down and a new year begins, many individuals find themselves grappling with the unsettling emotions brought on by the end of the holiday period. This essay will explore the challenges individuals face when readjusting to their regular routines after the holidays, particularly in relation to depression and relationships. The holiday season tends to disrupt daily schedules, creating a sense of freedom and relaxation. People are often granted time off from work and school, allowing them to spend more time with family and friends. This break from routine can provide respite from the daily pressures and stressors that plague individuals throughout the year. Once the holidays end, individuals are forced to return to the demands of their regular lives, which can be deflating. This abrupt disruption to the holiday-induced euphoria can lead to feelings of depression. The stark contrast between the joy and excitement of the holiday season and the mundane reality of everyday life can leave individuals feeling demotivated and disheartened. As they struggle to readjust to their regular routines, they may experience a sense of emptiness, as the holiday spirit dissipates, and the cozy atmosphere of family gatherings fades away. This emotional downturn can be exacerbated by the societal pressure to embrace the "new year, new me" mentality, which can make individuals feel overwhelmed by the need for transformation and growth. Relationships can also be significantly affected by the end of the holiday season. During the holiday period, individuals often spend increased amounts of time with their loved ones, strengthening bonds and creating cherished memories. Once routines return to normal, these individuals may find themselves grappling with a sense of loss and disconnection. The absence of constant companionship and the return to separate work or school schedules can strain relationships. The increased demands of daily life can leave individuals with less time and energy to devote to their loved ones, leading to feelings of neglect or abandonment. The holiday season can create unrealistic expectations for relationships, with idyllic portrayals of love and happiness perpetuated by the media. When these expectations are not met, individuals may become disillusioned and dissatisfied with their relationships. The end of the holiday season can be a tumultuous time for many individuals as they navigate the challenges associated with readjusting to their regular routines. Depression can arise from the sudden loss of joy and the harsh contrast between the holiday festivities and the mundane reality of everyday life. Relationships can also suffer as the demands of daily life limit the time and energy individuals can devote to their loved ones. Understanding these challenges and actively addressing them can help individuals transition more smoothly into their post-holiday routines.

HOOK

The holiday season is often described as a joyful time, filled with family, friends, and festivities.

For many individuals, the end of the holiday season signifies the return to their regular routines and responsibilities, which can lead to feelings of depression and anxiety. One reason for this is the loss of social connections and the sense of community that often accompanies the holiday season. During this time, individuals are surrounded by loved ones and have the opportunity to engage in various activities and traditions. From family gatherings to holiday parties, these events provide a sense of belonging and togetherness that can be difficult to replicate in everyday life. As the holiday season comes to a close and people go back to their normal lives, they may find themselves feeling lonely and isolated, especially if they do not have strong support networks outside of the holiday season.

The abrupt transition from a relaxed and festive atmosphere to the demands of work or school can be highly stressful. While the holiday season often allows for downtime and relaxation, the post-holiday period can be filled with deadlines, responsibilities, and expectations. This sudden shift in routine can be overwhelming and lead to a sense of anxiety and pressure. The pressure to start the new year on a high note and meet personal or professional goals can add to the stress and create unrealistic expectations for oneself. The contrast between the joy and excitement of the holiday season and the looming demands of everyday life can contribute to feelings of inadequacy and sadness.

The holiday season is often associated with indulgence and excess, from delicious food to lavish gifts and extravagant experiences. This can trigger a sense of loss and disappointment as individuals come to terms with the end of these indulgences and return to more moderate and mundane routines. The excitement and anticipation that come with the holiday season are replaced with the ordinary and mundane aspects of daily life, which can be disheartening for some.

The end of the holiday season can bring about a range of emotions, including depression, anxiety, and readjustment difficulties. The loss of social connections, the stress of transitioning back to everyday routines, and the contrast between indulgence and moderation can all contribute to these feelings. It is important for individuals to acknowledge and address these emotions, seeking support when needed and finding ways to incorporate joy and fulfillment into their post-holiday lives. By recognizing the challenges that may arise during this time, individuals can better navigate the transition and find ways to maintain their mental well-being.

BACKGROUND

For many individuals, the post-holiday period can bring about feelings of depression, strain on relationships, and difficulties in adjusting back to their regular routines.

The festive holiday season is often associated with joy, love, and a sense of community. It offers a break from the daily grind and provides an opportunity for individuals to relax, unwind, and replenish their energy. Once the holidays come to an end, the post-holiday period can be a challenging time for many people. The transition from a carefree, joyful atmosphere to the reality of routine life can be overwhelming and lead to feelings of sadness and loneliness. Some individuals may experience post-holiday depression, commonly known as the "post-holiday blues," which is characterized by a temporary downturn in mood, low energy levels, and a general sense of dissatisfaction.

The post-holiday period can also strain relationships. During the holiday season, individuals often spend an increased amount of time with their loved ones, creating precious memories and deepening their bonds. When the holidays end, the demands of work, school, and other responsibilities can lead to a decrease in quality time spent together. This sudden shift can create tension and conflict within relationships, as individuals struggle to readjust to their routines and find a harmonious balance between their personal and professional lives. The financial strain of the holiday season can further exacerbate relationship difficulties, as individuals may find themselves facing increased stress and conflicts related to money management.

In addition to depression and relationship strain, readjusting to regular routines after the holidays can pose significant challenges for many individuals. The holiday period often brings disruptions to daily schedules, including changes in sleep patterns, altered mealtimes, and reduced physical activity. Once the holidays are over, individuals may struggle to revert back to their regular routines, leading to feelings of disorientation, fatigue, and decreased productivity. The pressure to set and achieve personal and professional goals in the new year can add to the stress and overwhelm individuals even further.

While the holidays offer an exhilarating break from the daily routine, the post-holiday period can bring about a mix of emotions, strains on relationships, and difficulties in adjusting back to regular routines. It is important for individuals to understand these potential challenges and actively work towards managing them. Seeking support from loved ones, practicing self-care, and gradually easing back into one's routine can help alleviate the negative feelings associated with the post-holiday period. By acknowledging and addressing these issues, individuals can navigate the post-holiday period with resilience and ultimately find a sense of balance and well-being in their lives.

THESIS STATEMENT

This essay explores the impact of post-holiday depression, relationship challenges, and the process of readjusting after the holiday season. Post-holiday depression is a common phenomenon that affects many individuals, and its impact should not be underestimated. The excitement and joy of the holiday season can abruptly come to an end, leaving individuals feeling empty and sad. The sudden shift from holiday festivities to the routine of everyday life can be overwhelming for some, leading to a sense of post-holiday depression. This emotional state can be characterized by feelings of sadness, lethargy, and a lack of motivation. The pressure of returning to work or school after a period of relaxation can further exacerbate these symptoms. The stress and demands of daily life can seem even more daunting after the holiday season, making it challenging for individuals to readjust. The holiday season is often a time to gather with family and loved ones, which can bring immense joy and happiness. It can also expose and intensify existing relationship challenges. Spending an extended period of time with family can bring unresolved conflicts and tensions to the surface. The pressure to meet expectations and maintain a harmonious atmosphere can strain relationships, leading to increased conflict and dissatisfaction. The holiday season can highlight feelings of loneliness for individuals who do not have strong support systems. This can create a sense of isolation and further contribute to post-holiday depression. The period following the holidays is crucial for individuals to address these relationship challenges and seek resolutions, as neglecting them can have long-lasting negative impacts.

The process of readjusting after the holiday season can be a complex and gradual one. The transition from a relaxed and leisurely routine to one filled with responsibilities and obligations can be overwhelming. It takes time to adapt to the demands of work, school, and everyday life after a period of indulgence and relaxation. Readjustment may involve setting new goals and expectations, as well as establishing a sense of structure and routine. This process can be particularly challenging for individuals who struggle with change or find it difficult to cope with stress. Support systems and effective coping mechanisms are crucial during this period to help individuals navigate the readjustment process successfully.

Post-holiday depression, relationship challenges, and the process of readjusting after the holiday season have a significant impact on individuals. The sudden shift from the excitement of the holiday season to the routine of everyday life can be emotionally challenging, leading to feelings of sadness and post-holiday depression. Relationship challenges that are exposed during this time can strain familial and social connections. The readjustment process involves adapting to the demands of work, school, and everyday life after a period of relaxation, which can be overwhelming for many individuals. Recognizing these challenges and seeking appropriate support can help individuals effectively navigate this period and transition back to a stable routine. The holiday season, with its festivities and celebrations, often serves as a welcomed distraction from the demands of everyday life. As the decorations are packed away and the holiday spirit fades, many individuals find themselves struggling to readjust to their regular routines. For individuals who suffer from depression, this period of transition can be particularly challenging. The sudden change from a season of joy and togetherness to one of isolation and monotony can exacerbate feelings of sadness and hopelessness. The social interactions that were once abundant during the holidays tend to dwindle, leaving those with depression feeling even more isolated. The pressure to return to work or school after a break can feel overwhelming, as the responsibilities and demands of daily life become a heavy weight on already vulnerable shoulders.

The readjustment period after the holidays can also have a profound impact on relationships. During the festive season, individuals often prioritize spending time with loved ones, taking part in shared activities and creating lasting memories. Once the holidays are over, people tend to retreat back into their individual lives, often neglecting the connections that were strengthened during the holiday season. This neglect can lead to feelings of resentment and loneliness, as individuals may feel that the effort and time they invested in their relationships during the holiday season were in vain.

To combat the negative effects of readjustment after the holidays, it is essential for individuals to prioritize self-care and maintain open lines of communication with loved ones. Engaging in activities that bring joy and fulfillment can help combat the post-holiday blues and counteract feelings of sadness and loneliness. Whether it is practicing a hobby, exercising, or simply taking time for oneself, self-care can serve as a powerful tool in alleviating symptoms of depression and promoting overall well-being. Maintaining open lines of communication with loved ones can help preserve the connections that were strengthened during the holiday season. Regular check-ins, phone calls, or even planning future gatherings can help maintain the sense of togetherness and support that characterized the festive season. Understanding that the readjustment period may be challenging for both oneself and others can foster empathy and facilitate a smoother transition back to regular routines.

The readjustment period after the holidays can impact individuals differently based on their mental health, affecting both their emotional well-being and relationships. For those with depression, the return to routine can intensify feelings of sadness and isolation. Relationships, once nurtured during the festive season, can suffer as individuals retreat into their individual lives. By prioritizing self-care and maintaining open lines of communication, individuals can navigate this readjustment period with greater resilience and maintain the sense of connection and support that characterized the holiday season.

II. POST-HOLIDAY DEPRESSION

Post-holiday depression is not just limited to individuals; it can also have a significant impact on relationships. After weeks of holiday festivities and spending more quality time together, the sudden shift back to reality and routine can strain a relationship. The holiday period offers a unique opportunity for couples to bond and create cherished memories. Coming back from this euphoric state and facing the reality of work, responsibilities, and less leisure time can lead to disappointment and frustration. During the holidays, couples often have more time to engage in activities they enjoy, such as traveling, exploring new places, and spending uninterrupted time together. But once the holidays are over, the constraints of daily life start to take precedence again. The busy schedules and different priorities of each partner can create a sense of disconnection and result in post-holiday blues. The financial strain that often accompanies the holiday season can add another layer of stress to the relationship. Couples who overspent or went into debt during the holidays may experience increased tension and conflict, leading to a sense of dissatisfaction and discontentment. It is crucial during this time to communicate openly and empathetically with your partner, expressing your emotions and understanding their experiences as well. Both partners need to acknowledge and validate each other's feelings, providing support and reassurance during this readjustment period. Setting realistic expectations and finding new ways to connect and enjoy each other's company can also alleviate the post-holiday blues. For instance, planning regular date nights or finding shared hobbies can help reignite the spark in the relationship. Taking care of oneself by engaging in self-care practices and maintaining a healthy lifestyle can positively influence relationships. When individuals feel good about themselves, they are more likely to bring positivity and joy into their interactions with their partner. While post-holiday depression can undoubtedly put a strain on relationships, it is essential to remember that these feelings are temporary. With time, patience, and open communication, couples can navigate through this period and find a healthy balance between the joy of the holidays and the demands of everyday life. Understanding that it is natural to feel a sense of sadness or loss after the holidays can help individuals normalize their emotions and be more compassionate towards themselves and their partners. By acknowledging the impact of post-holiday depression on relationships and taking proactive steps to overcome it, couples can adapt to the return to routine and create a stronger, healthier bond.

DEFINITION AND SYMPTOMS

Post-holiday depression refers to a state of sadness or emotional distress experienced after the holiday season.

Post-holiday depression, also known as post-holiday blues, is characterized by a feeling of sadness or emotional distress experienced after the holiday season. This condition is not uncommon and affects a significant number of individuals who find it challenging to transition back to their regular routines after the festive period. Symptoms of post-holiday depression can vary from person to person but often include feelings of sadness, irritability, fatigue, decreased motivation, and a general sense of emptiness. Individuals may experience difficulty concentrating on tasks, a loss of appetite, changes in sleep patterns, and a lack of interest in activities they previously enjoyed. These symptoms can be particularly distressing for college students who may be facing additional stressors such as exams, deadlines, and the pressure to perform academically. College life already comes with its own set of challenges, and the post-holiday period can exacerbate feelings of anxiety and depression. The transition from a relaxed and carefree break to the demands of daily college life can be overwhelming, leading to a sense of despair and a decline in overall emotional well-being. The contrast between the excitement and socialization of the holiday season and the isolation and academic pressures of college can further contribute to post-holiday depression. The lack of contact with close friends and family, coupled with the absence of festive activities, can intensify feelings of loneliness and sadness. It is essential for college students to recognize and address these symptoms to prevent them from progressing into more severe forms of depression. Seeking support from friends, family, and mental health professionals can be instrumental in managing post-holiday depression. Engaging in self-care activities such as exercise, meditation, and maintaining a healthy diet can also help alleviate some of the symptoms associated with this condition. Developing a routine and setting achievable goals can provide structure and a sense of purpose, helping individuals regain control and adjust to their regular college life. Fostering and maintaining social connections, whether through in-person interactions or virtual platforms, can foster a sense of belonging and alleviate feelings of isolation. By recognizing the signs of post-holiday depression and taking proactive steps to address it, college students can not only manage their emotional well-being but also thrive in their academic pursuits.

CAUSES

Factors such as decreased social interaction, financial strain, and unmet expectations can contribute to post-holiday depression. One major cause of post-holiday depression is decreased social interaction. During the holiday season, individuals tend to spend more time with friends and family, attending parties, and engaging in various social activities. This increased social interaction provides a sense of belonging, emotional support, and joy. Once the holiday season concludes, these interactions often decrease, and individuals may find themselves feeling lonely and disconnected. The sudden absence of social engagement can be particularly challenging for those who already struggle with feelings of isolation or have limited social support networks. Another contributing factor to post-holiday depression is financial strain. The holiday season is often associated with increased spending on gifts, travel, and social events. Many individuals may feel pressured to participate in gift exchanges or lavish celebrations, leading to financial burdens. Once the holidays are over, the reality of excessive spending sets in, leaving individuals feeling stressed and overwhelmed. The financial strain resulting from holiday expenses can create anxiety and feelings of regret, exacerbating the sense of post-holiday depression. Unmet expectations can also play a significant role in post-holiday depression. The holiday season is often portrayed as a time of happiness, joy, and togetherness in the media. This idealized image can create unrealistic expectations for individuals, leading to disappointment when reality falls short. Whether it be tensions between family members, failed attempts at creating perfect holiday memories, or unfulfilled expectations for meaningful connections, unmet expectations can evoke feelings of sadness, frustration, and loneliness. These negative emotions can persist even after the holidays have ended, contributing to post-holiday depression.

Post-holiday depression can be attributed to several causes that influence an individual's well-being and emotional state. The decreased social interaction that follows the end of the holiday season can leave individuals feeling isolated and disconnected. Financial strain resulting from excessive spending during the holidays can also contribute to feelings of stress and overwhelm. Unmet expectations surrounding the holiday season can lead to disappointment and a sense of sadness. It is essential to recognize these factors and take proactive steps to minimize their impact. Engaging in fulfilling social activities, creating a realistic holiday budget, and managing expectations can help individuals navigate the post-holiday period and reduce the risk of experiencing depression. By understanding these causes and actively addressing them, individuals can better manage their mental health and transition back to their routines successfully.

CONSEQUENCES

Post-holiday depression may lead to decreased productivity, withdrawal from social activities, and a decline in overall well-being. After the festivities and excitement of the holiday season come to an end, many individuals find themselves facing a wave of post-holiday depression. This emotional state can have several detrimental consequences on various aspects of an individual's life. One of the most noticeable effects is a decrease in productivity. The lack of motivation and energy that comes with post-holiday depression often leads to difficulties in focusing and completing tasks efficiently. This decline in productivity can have negative consequences in both academic and professional settings, as individuals struggle to meet expectations and fulfill responsibilities. Post-holiday depression often causes individuals to withdraw from social activities. The contrast between the lively gatherings and social interactions of the holiday season and the quiet, empty days that follow can be difficult to bear. Consequently, individuals may feel a sense of isolation and disconnection from others, leading them to avoid social engagements altogether. This withdrawal from social activities can further exacerbate the feelings of loneliness and sadness associated with post-holiday depression. The impact of post-holiday depression on an individual's overall well-being cannot be overlooked. This emotional state can manifest in physical symptoms such as fatigue, insomnia, and changes in appetite. The combination of these physical and emotional symptoms can lead to a decline in an individual's overall sense of well-being. The ongoing sadness and lack of motivation can make it challenging for individuals to engage in self-care activities, further perpetuating the cycle of negative emotions. Thus, post-holiday depression takes a toll on an individual's mental, emotional, and physical health, affecting their overall quality of life. The consequences of post-holiday depression can be far-reaching and significant. The decrease in productivity, withdrawal from social activities, and decline in overall well-being can have detrimental effects on an individual's personal and professional life. It is crucial to recognize and address post-holiday depression to minimize its impact and provide individuals with the necessary support and resources to navigate this challenging period effectively. By acknowledging the consequences and taking steps towards self-care and seeking help if necessary, individuals can regain their sense of well-being and adjust to their routines after the holidays. Readjusting to the routine after the holiday season can have significant impacts on an individual's mental health and relationships. The post-holiday blues or depression can be caused by several factors, including the end of the festive period, return to work or school, and financial stress. These feelings of sadness and hopelessness can be intensified by the pressure to conform to societal expectations and the comparison to others. The decline in social activities and the loss of the support and comfort from loved ones during the holiday season can further contribute to the sense of loneliness and isolation. As a result, individuals may struggle to cope with the sudden change in their daily lives, leading to the deteriorating quality of their relationships and overall well-being. There are strategies that can help alleviate these challenges and promote a smoother transition. Firstly, individuals can manage their expectations by setting realistic goals and priorities, recognizing that it is normal to experience a drop in mood and motivation after the holidays. Engaging in self-care practices such as exercise, getting sufficient sleep, and maintaining a balanced diet can also help improve one's mental health and overall well-being. Individuals should seek support from their loved ones, friends, or professional therapists, as talking about their emotions and receiving validation can be beneficial in coping with the readjustment process. Implementing small changes in one's routine and incorporating enjoyable activities can also help counteract feelings of monotony and provide a sense of purpose and fulfillment. It is important to remember that everyone's experience is unique, and comparing oneself to others can be counterproductive. Instead, individuals should focus on their own progress and take pride in small accomplishments along their journey. By taking these steps, individuals can navigate the post-holiday readjustment period more effectively, improving their mental health and strengthening their relationships. Understanding the challenges and taking proactive measures to support oneself can ultimately lead to a smoother transition into the routine and mitigate the negative impacts of the post-holiday period.

III. RELATIONSHIP CHALLENGES

One of the biggest challenges that individuals face after the holidays is reestablishing and readjusting their relationships. When the holiday season comes to an end, everyone goes back to their usual routines and responsibilities, which can impact the dynamics of their relationships. For couples, the transition from the excitement and togetherness of the holidays to the mundane everyday life can be particularly challenging. Research has shown that after the holidays, couples often experience a decrease in relationship satisfaction and an increase in conflict (Wickham & Seawell, 2020). This may be due to a variety of factors, such as unrealistically high expectations during the holiday season, financial stress from holiday expenses, or simply the letdown of returning to normalcy after a period of heightened emotions and experiences.

The holiday season tends to bring families together, and the end of this period can result in feelings of loneliness and disconnection. After spending quality time with loved ones, individuals may struggle to adjust to a quieter, more solitary lifestyle. This can be particularly challenging for individuals who live far away from their families or have strained relationships with them. The end of the holidays may intensify feelings of homesickness or a sense of not belonging. Such emotional strain can affect not only an individual's mental well-being but also their ability to engage in healthy relationships with others.

The readjustment after the holidays can also impact friendships and social connections. During the holiday season, people often have a busier social calendar filled with parties, gatherings, and events. Once the holiday season ends, individuals may find themselves having less time or energy to maintain these friendships. The expectations of constant connection and interaction that are present during the holidays can set unrealistic standards for relationships, leading to disappointment and strained friendships. The period after the holidays can pose several challenges to individuals in terms of their relationships. Couples may experience a decrease in relationship satisfaction and an increase in conflict, while individuals may feel lonely or disconnected from their families. The readjustment after the holidays may strain friendships and social connections. It is important for individuals to be aware of these challenges and take proactive steps to address them. This may involve openly communicating with their partners about their feelings and expectations, making an effort to maintain connections with loved ones, and setting realistic boundaries and priorities in their friendships. By acknowledging and actively addressing the challenges that arise after the holidays, individuals can navigate this transitional period and ensure that their relationships remain strong and healthy.

STRAIN ON ROMANTIC RELATIONSHIPS

The intense togetherness experienced during the holidays can cause relationship tension and conflicts.

During the holiday season, couples often spend a significant amount of time together, which can lead to strain on their romantic relationships. The intense togetherness experienced during the holidays can cause relationship tension and conflicts. This can be due to a variety of factors, including the pressure to create the perfect holiday experience, dealing with stressful family dynamics, and the increased expectations for couples to spend quality time together. For many couples, the holidays can be a time of heightened emotions and stress, which can result in arguments, disagreements, and overall tension in the relationship. The pressure to meet the expectations of family members and friends can add to the strain on relationships. Couples may feel obligated to attend numerous social events and split their time between different family gatherings, leading to feelings of overwhelm and exhaustion. This can leave little room for quality time and connection between partners, adding to the strain on the relationship. Holiday traditions and rituals can also contribute to relationship tension. Each partner may have different expectations and desires for how to celebrate the holidays, and these differences can lead to conflict if not adequately addressed and compromised upon. The added financial strain of holiday expenses can also contribute to relationship conflicts. The pressure to buy gifts, host parties, and participate in other holiday-related expenditures can lead to disagreements about money and financial stress within the relationship. It is essential for couples to communicate openly and honestly about their expectations and desires during the holiday season to minimize strain on their relationship. Setting realistic expectations and prioritizing self-care can also be beneficial in navigating the intense togetherness of the holidays. Implementing strategies such as taking breaks from family gatherings, scheduling alone time, and practicing stress-reducing activities together can help couples manage the strain on their relationship during the holiday season. Couples should be mindful of each other's emotional well-being and actively work to support and validate each other in navigating the stressors of the holiday season. By recognizing and addressing the potential strain on their relationship, couples can better navigate the intense togetherness experienced during the holidays and maintain a healthy and fulfilling romantic partnership.

CONFLICT RESOLUTION

Effective communication and managing expectations can help address relationship challenges and prevent long-lasting damage. Effective communication and managing expectations are essential aspects of conflict resolution and can play a crucial role in addressing relationship challenges and preventing long-lasting damage. When conflicts arise, it is crucial to engage in open and honest communication to understand each other's perspectives and find common ground. This communication should be empathetic and non-judgmental, allowing both parties to express their feelings and concerns without fear of criticism or retaliation. By actively listening to one another and acknowledging each other's emotions, individuals can foster a sense of mutual understanding and empathy, which can help in finding constructive resolutions. Managing expectations is a vital component of conflict resolution. Often, conflicts arise due to unmet expectations or unrealistic assumptions about the other person's behavior or actions. By clearly articulating and discussing expectations from the outset, individuals can avoid misunderstandings and navigate potential conflict triggers. This can be achieved by engaging in transparent and proactive communication, discussing each other's needs, and finding compromise or alternative solutions when necessary. Recognizing that both parties have their unique perspectives and desires can also help in adjusting expectations and finding middle ground. Addressing relationship challenges in a timely manner is crucial to prevent long-lasting damage. Unresolved conflicts tend to grow over time, leading to resentment and emotional distance in relationships. By approaching conflict resolution promptly and directly, individuals can prevent minor disagreements from escalating into major issues. This requires a willingness to confront challenging situations head-on and take ownership of one's own contributions to the conflict. Being proactive in resolving conflicts not only fosters healthier and more satisfying relationships but also contributes to personal growth and self-awareness. Effective communication and managing expectations are vital for conflict resolution and preventing long-lasting damage in relationships. By engaging in open and honest communication, individuals can understand each other's perspectives, express their feelings, and find common ground.

Managing expectations through transparent and proactive communication helps to avoid misunderstandings and navigate potential conflict triggers. Addressing relationship challenges promptly and directly is essential to prevent minor disagreements from escalating into major issues and fostering healthier and more satisfying relationships. Conflict resolution through effective communication and responsible expectation management contributes to personal growth, mutual understanding, and the overall well-being of individuals and their relationships.

STRENGTHENING BONDS

Utilizing shared experiences and applying stress management techniques can help couples reconnect and improve their relationship. The holiday season can often be a stressful time for couples, with family obligations, financial pressures, and increased expectations. These factors can take a toll on a relationship and lead to feelings of disconnect and strain. By actively engaging in shared experiences and applying stress management techniques, couples can reestablish a sense of connection and rekindle their love and intimacy. One effective way to strengthen bonds is by participating in activities together. Whether it be going on a romantic weekend getaway, cooking together, or engaging in a shared hobby, these shared experiences can serve as a reminder of the joy and love that initially brought the couple together. Engaging in activities together fosters a sense of teamwork and solidarity, allowing couples to navigate challenges and create lasting memories together. Couples can benefit from practicing stress management techniques together. The holiday season often amplifies stress levels, and these heightened stress levels can strain the relationship. By implementing stress management techniques such as deep breathing exercises, meditation, or engaging in physical activity together, couples can effectively manage stress and promote a harmonious environment. Taking time to relax and unwind as a couple allows for deeper connection and understanding, as both partners feel supported and cared for. It is essential for couples to communicate openly and honestly about their emotions and needs. During the holiday season, it can be easy for couples to bury their feelings and focus solely on attending to the needs of others. This lack of communication can lead to misunderstandings and resentment, further deteriorating the relationship. It is imperative for couples to create a safe space for open and honest communication, where both partners can express their feelings and concerns. By actively listening and empathizing with one another, couples can rebuild trust and strengthen their emotional bond. Seeking professional help can also be a valuable resource for couples looking to reconnect and improve their relationship. Therapists can provide guidance and support, offering strategies and tools to foster better communication, manage stress, and navigate the challenges that arise during the post-holiday period. Therapy provides a neutral space for couples to address deep-rooted issues and work towards mutual growth and happiness. By committing to strengthening their bond and utilizing these strategies, couples can navigate the post-holiday slump and embark on a path towards a healthier, more fulfilling relationship.

While the holiday season is often described as a time of joy and happiness, for many individuals, it can also be a period of increased stress and mental health challenges. As the holidays come to an end and individuals return to their daily routines, they may experience feelings of depression, difficulties in their relationships, and the need to readjust back to normalcy. One reason for these challenges is the contrast between the holiday season and the regular daily life. The holidays are often filled with social gatherings, family reunions, and celebrations, creating an atmosphere of togetherness and happiness. When individuals return to their usual routines, they may find themselves feeling isolated and lonely. The stark contrast between the joyous holiday period and the mundane nature of everyday life can be a trigger for depression, as it can create a sense of emptiness and sadness. The pressures of the holiday season, such as the expectations of gift-giving and hosting gatherings, can lead to financial stress and exhaustion. This can contribute to feelings of overwhelm and burnout, making it even more challenging to readjust to everyday life. The holiday season can bring about significant changes in relationships. During this time, individuals may spend more time with loved ones, creating memories and strengthening bonds. As the holidays end, people often return to their separate lives, and the intensity of those connections fades away. This transition can lead to feelings of loneliness and disconnection within relationships. The abrupt shift from constant togetherness to the realities of distance and independent routines can strain even the closest relationships. Communication and effort are essential to navigate this period, as partners and loved ones must establish new routines for maintaining connection and supporting each other through this transition. To readjust to everyday life, individuals need to establish a new sense of normalcy after the holidays. Creating a structure and routine can help provide stability and a sense of purpose. Setting small, achievable goals can also provide a sense of accomplishment and motivation. Taking care of one's physical and mental well-being is crucial during this time. Engaging in activities that bring joy and practicing self-care can help counteract the post-holiday blues. Seeking support from friends, family, or mental health professionals can be beneficial in managing the challenges of readjustment. By acknowledging and addressing these feelings and actively working towards healthier coping mechanisms, individuals can navigate this period of transition more effectively.

The end of the holiday season can bring about depression, challenges in relationships, and the need to readjust to normalcy. The contrast between the holiday period and daily life, the changes in relationships, and the pressures of readjustment all contribute to this difficulty. By recognizing and addressing these challenges, individuals can make healthy choices, establish new routines, and seek support to successfully transition back into everyday life.

IV. ADJUSTING TO ROUTINE

One of the biggest challenges that individuals face after the holiday season is readjusting to their routines. The holiday season often disrupts the regular daily schedule, with many people taking time off work and school to celebrate with family and friends. As a result, getting back into the swing of things can feel overwhelming and even disorienting. The sudden shift from relaxation and indulgence to a structured and disciplined routine can trigger feelings of anxiety and sadness. This adjustment period is particularly difficult for those who struggle with depression, as the return to routine can exacerbate their symptoms. For individuals with depression, the holiday season often provides a much-needed reprieve from the pressures and stressors of everyday life. The festive atmosphere and time spent with loved ones can temporarily alleviate feelings of loneliness and despair. When the holidays come to an end and routines resume, these individuals may find themselves confronted with the stark reality of their everyday lives. The return to work or school can feel overwhelming, and they may struggle to find motivation or interest in their daily activities. This can further exacerbate their depressive symptoms and make it difficult for them to adjust to the demands of their routine.

In addition to the challenges posed by depression, readjusting to routine after the holidays can also strain personal relationships. During the holiday season, individuals often spend an extended period of time with family and friends, creating memories and strengthening bonds. As the holidays draw to a close, everyone goes back to their respective lives, and maintaining those connections becomes more challenging. The transition from constantly being surrounded by loved ones to spending most of one's time alone can lead to feelings of loneliness and isolation, which can negatively impact one's mental health.

To effectively cope with the adjustment period after the holidays, it is important to implement self-care strategies and prioritize mental well-being. This may include establishing a consistent sleep schedule, practicing regular exercise, and engaging in activities that bring joy and fulfillment. Maintaining open and honest communication with loved ones can help alleviate feelings of loneliness and isolation. Sharing one's struggles and seeking support from trusted individuals can make the transition back to routine more manageable.

Readjusting to routine after the holiday season can be challenging, particularly for individuals with depression. The sudden shift from relaxation to structure can trigger feelings of anxiety and sadness, exacerbating depressive symptoms. The return to routine can strain personal relationships, leading to feelings of loneliness and isolation. By implementing self-care strategies and maintaining open communication with loved ones, individuals can better navigate the adjustment period and promote their mental well-being.

DIFFICULTY TRANSITIONING

After weeks of holiday celebrations, individuals often struggle to adjust back to their regular schedules and routines.

Difficulty transitioning: After weeks of holiday celebrations, individuals often struggle to adjust back to their regular schedules and routines. The festive atmosphere with its lively social engagements, indulgent food, and relaxed time spent with loved ones creates a stark contrast to the mundane demands of everyday life. This sudden shift from joyful festivities to monotonous routines can generate feelings of sadness, lethargy, and even depression, commonly referred to as the post-holiday blues. It is not uncommon for individuals to experience a sense of emptiness or loneliness as they return to their normal routines and find themselves missing the warmth and joy of the holiday season. The abrupt change in social dynamics can also be challenging, especially for extroverted individuals who thrive in the company of others. The absence of constant family gatherings and the hustle and bustle of holiday parties can leave individuals feeling disconnected and isolated.

In addition to the emotional toll, the return to normalcy after the holidays can also pose practical challenges. For many, the holiday season means a break from work or school, allowing time for rest, relaxation, and rejuvenation. Consequently, transitioning back to the demands of academic or professional life can be daunting and overwhelming. The return to strict schedules, deadlines, and responsibilities can easily trigger stress and anxiety. The indulgent eating and drinking that often characterize the holiday season can lead to a disruption in healthy eating habits, making it difficult to revert to a balanced and nutritious diet. This sudden shift in lifestyle can have negative implications for physical well-being, compounding the emotional difficulties already experienced during this period of readjustment.

The pressure to set resolutions for the new year can exacerbate feelings of anxiety and inadequacy. With the arrival of January, individuals are bombarded with messages promoting self-improvement and the need to set goals for the upcoming year. This societal pressure can heighten the sense of failure or disappointment if individuals have not achieved their desired goals or resolutions from the previous year. The fear of falling short in personal and professional pursuits can cast a shadow over the early days of the new year, further intensifying the difficulty of transitioning back to regular routines.

The post-holiday period can be a challenging time for individuals as they struggle to readjust to their regular schedules and routines. The emotional toll, practical challenges, and societal pressures all contribute to the difficulty experienced during this transitional period. Recognizing the commonality of these struggles and seeking support from loved ones or professionals can help individuals navigate this challenging period more effectively. By understanding and addressing these difficulties, it is possible to make the transition back to normalcy in a healthier and more positive manner.

ESTABLISHING A SCHEDULE

Developing a structured daily routine can provide a sense of stability and ease the transition process.

Establishing a schedule is crucial when it comes to transitioning back to routine after the holidays. Developing a structured daily routine can provide a sense of stability and ease the transition process. During the holidays, many individuals experience a break from their regular schedules, leading to a lack of structure in their lives. They may have stayed up late, slept in, and had irregular mealtimes. As a result, returning to a structured routine can be challenging, and it may take some time to readjust. By establishing a schedule, individuals can regain a sense of order and normalcy in their lives. Having a daily routine helps to establish a sense of stability. When individuals have a set routine, they know what to expect each day. This predictability can provide a sense of security and reduce anxiety. By having a regular waking up and bedtime routine, individuals can regulate their sleep patterns, ensuring they get enough rest. This can have a significant impact on mental health and overall well-being. Having specific times for meals and exercise can contribute to physical health, as it promotes regularity and consistency. Establishing a schedule can ease the transition process and make it more manageable. Going from a carefree holiday mindset to a structured routine can be overwhelming, and individuals may feel disoriented and stressed. By setting a schedule, they can gradually reintroduce structure back into their lives. It allows them to take small steps towards readjustment, making the process smoother and less daunting. By breaking down tasks and activities into manageable chunks, individuals can focus on one thing at a time, reducing feelings of being overwhelmed. A structured daily routine also promotes productivity and time management. By allocating specific time slots for different tasks, individuals can prioritize their responsibilities and efficiently manage their time. This can help them stay organized, meet deadlines, and achieve their goals. A schedule can also provide a sense of accomplishment as individuals complete tasks and see progress throughout the day. This can boost motivation and confidence, leading to increased productivity.

Establishing a schedule is crucial for individuals facing the transition back to routine after the holidays. By developing a structured daily routine, individuals can regain stability and ease the readjustment process. Having a regular routine provides predictability and reduces anxiety. It helps individuals regulate their sleep patterns, maintain physical health, and establish a sense of order in their lives. Setting a schedule promotes productivity, time management, and a sense of accomplishment. A structured routine is essential for individuals to smoothly transition back to routine after indulging in the holiday festivities.

COPING STRATEGIES

Engaging in self-care activities, setting realistic goals, and seeking social support are essential for successfully adapting to post-holiday routines. Coping strategies play a crucial role in helping individuals adapt to post-holiday routines. Engaging in self-care activities can be an effective way to alleviate stress and maintain overall well-being. Taking time to engage in activities that bring joy and relaxation, such as practicing Mindfulness , exercising, or enjoying hobbies, can help individuals recharge and refocus their energy. Setting realistic goals is another important coping strategy that can aid in the transition back to routine. By breaking down larger tasks into smaller, manageable goals, individuals can set themselves up for success and avoid becoming overwhelmed.

This approach allows them to prioritize and tackle tasks one step at a time, ultimately leading to a sense of accomplishment and empowerment. Seeking social support is yet another vital coping strategy during this period. Connecting with others who are going through similar experiences or with supportive friends and family members can provide a sense of belonging and understanding. Sharing feelings, experiences, and concerns with trusted individuals can not only help alleviate stress but also provide insight and guidance from others who have successfully navigated similar transitions. Receiving encouragement and reassurance from loved ones can boost self-confidence and motivation. Engaging in self-care activities, setting realistic goals, and seeking social support are essential for successfully adapting to post-holiday routines. These coping strategies provide individuals with the tools necessary to navigate the challenges that may arise during this time. By prioritizing self-care, individuals can better manage stress, avoid burnout, and maintain their emotional well-being. Setting realistic goals ensures that individuals can effectively structure their time and accomplish tasks without feeling overwhelmed. Seeking social support allows individuals to lean on others for guidance, encouragement, and understanding, ultimately helping them feel supported and less alone. As individuals implement and prioritize these coping strategies, they can effectively transition back to their daily routines, nurturing their mental health and fostering a sense of balance and fulfillment in their lives. One common issue that many people experience after going through the holiday season is a sense of sadness or depression. The holidays often bring with them a sense of excitement and joy, but once they are over, individuals may find themselves feeling down and lacking motivation. This phenomenon, commonly known as the "post-holiday blues," can have a significant impact on one's mental health and well-being. The abrupt end to the festivities and return to the mundane routine of everyday life can be quite overwhelming. This feeling of sadness can be heightened by the fact that the holiday season is often filled with social activities and spending time with loved ones. After experiencing such a high level of interaction and connection, it can be challenging to readjust to the more solitary and less eventful periods that follow. The holiday season is often associated with indulgence and excess, whether it be through food, alcohol, or material possessions. Once the holidays are over, many individuals may come face to face with the consequences of their choices, leading to feelings of guilt or regret. The pressure to live up to the expectations set by society during this time can also contribute to depressive feelings. People may compare their holiday experiences with those portrayed in movies or social media, leading to a sense of dissatisfaction with their own lives. This dissatisfaction can be especially pronounced in the realm of relationships. The holidays are often seen as a time for couples to strengthen their bond and create lasting memories together. Once the festivities end, couples may find themselves facing the reality of their relationship and any unresolved issues. The return to routine can magnify any pre-existing problems, leaving individuals feeling disconnected or unsatisfied in their partnerships. It is important to recognize that these post-holiday blues are a normal reaction to the changes in routine and social activities. It is crucial to address these feelings and take steps to mitigate their impact on mental health. Engaging in self-care, such as exercise, a healthy diet, and adequate sleep, can help regulate emotions and boost mood. Seeking support from friends, family, or mental health professionals can provide the necessary guidance and reassurance during this readjustment period. Developing a plan for the future and setting achievable goals can also help individuals regain a sense of purpose and motivation. By acknowledging and addressing these post-holiday blues, individuals can navigate the readjustment period with greater ease and ultimately find happiness and fulfillment in their day-to-day lives.

V. DEPRESSION RELAPSE

One of the crucial issues that individuals with depression may face after the holiday season is the potential for relapse. A relapse refers to the reoccurrence of depressive symptoms after a period of remission or improvement. While the holiday season can serve as a distraction and temporarily alleviate symptoms, once the festivities come to an end and routine sets back in, the risk of relapse becomes significant. Research suggests that individuals who experience depression have a higher likelihood of experiencing a relapse if they have a history of previous depressive episodes. There are several factors that can contribute to the relapse of depression after the holiday season. First and foremost, the social support systems that individuals rely on during the holidays may no longer be as readily available. The joyous gatherings and increased social interactions that occur during this time can provide comfort and a sense of belonging, acting as a buffer against depressive symptoms. Once the holidays are over, the individual may find themselves isolated and lacking the support they had grown accustomed to. This sudden withdrawal of social connection can lead to feelings of loneliness and exacerbate depressive symptoms. The post-holiday period often brings about a return to regular daily activities, such as work or school. The pressure and demands of these responsibilities can be overwhelming for someone already susceptible to depression, especially if they have not adequately adjusted to the change. The shift from a relaxed holiday routine to the demands of everyday life can cause feelings of stress, anxiety, and a sense of being overwhelmed. These negative emotions can contribute to the onset of depressive symptoms and increase the likelihood of relapse. Another factor that can contribute to the relapse of depression is the loss of the holiday season's positive emotions and experiences. The festivities and traditions associated with the holidays often bring joy, excitement, and a sense of purpose. These positive emotions can act as a temporary mood boost and provide individuals with a break from the depressive thoughts and feelings. Once the holiday season ends, individuals may struggle to find meaning and enjoyment in their everyday lives, leading to a sense of emptiness and the resurgence of depressive symptoms. The risk of depression relapse after the holiday season is a significant concern. Factors such as a lack of social support, the demands of daily responsibilities, and the loss of positive emotions can all contribute to the reoccurrence of depressive symptoms. Awareness of these potential triggers and implementing strategies to cope with them, such as maintaining regular social connections, practicing stress-management techniques, and seeking professional help, can be vital in preventing relapse and maintaining mental well-being during this readjustment period.

PREVALENCE OF RELAPSE

Post-holiday depression may trigger relapse for individuals with a history of depression. The transition from the holiday season to the regular routine can be a challenging period for many individuals, especially those who have a history of depression. The festivities, merriment, and overall sense of joy that accompany the holiday season can create a stark contrast to the more mundane and often stressful aspects of day-to-day life. As the holiday period comes to a close, individuals may find themselves grappling with a sense of emptiness or loneliness, which can exacerbate feelings of depression. This post-holiday slump can be particularly alarming for individuals who have experienced depression in the past, as it may act as a triggering factor for relapse. The holiday season tends to be filled with various social engagements and exciting activities, bringing people closer together and fostering a sense of connection. Once the holidays are over, these social interactions and distractions dissipate, leaving individuals susceptible to feelings of isolation and loneliness. For individuals who have battled depression, this sudden shift can be overwhelmingly challenging. The contrast between the joyous holiday festivities and the realities of day-to-day life can feel disheartening, leading to a relapse in depression symptoms. Another factor that contributes to the prevalence of relapse during the post-holiday period is the pressure to meet societal expectations surrounding the new year. Many individuals set high expectations for themselves, vowing to make significant changes or improvements in various aspects of their lives. When faced with the reality of returning to work, daily responsibilities, and the absence of the holiday excitement, these resolutions can feel overwhelming. The inability to meet these self-imposed expectations can trigger feelings of failure and disappointment, potentially leading to a relapse in depressive symptoms. The financial strain commonly associated with the holiday season can also contribute to post-holiday depression and subsequent relapse. Many individuals may find themselves facing substantial financial burdens after indulging in holiday shopping, festivities, and travel. The realization of the financial consequences can be distressing, especially for those who struggle to manage their finances or have previously experienced depression related to financial stress. This added pressure can intensify feelings of sadness and anxiety, increasing the likelihood of relapse. Given the prevalence of relapse during the post-holiday period, it is crucial for individuals with a history of depression to monitor their mental well-being closely. Seeking professional help, maintaining healthy habits, and engaging in self-care activities can be essential in navigating this challenging transition. Understanding the potential triggers and risk factors associated with post-holiday depression can empower individuals to proactively manage their mental health, reducing the likelihood of relapse and promoting overall well-being.

IDENTIFYING WARNING SIGNS

Recognizing early signs of relapse, such as changes in mood or sleep patterns, allows for early intervention and treatment.

Identifying warning signs of relapse is crucial for individuals with mental health disorders, especially after the holiday season. One key early sign that individuals should be vigilant for is changes in mood. Depression, for instance, may manifest as a persistent feeling of sadness or emptiness, irritability, or a loss of interest in activities that were once pleasurable. Recognizing these fluctuations in mood can allow for early intervention by seeking professional help, reaching out to support networks, or implementing coping strategies before the symptoms worsen. Similarly, changes in sleep patterns can serve as red flags as well. Insomnia, hypersomnia, or irregular sleep schedules are common symptoms of many mental health disorders, and they often exacerbate the emotional and cognitive symptoms associated with such conditions. By paying attention to these disruptions in sleep, individuals can take immediate actions to prevent relapse, such as establishing a regular sleep routine, practicing relaxation techniques before bed, or seeking medical advice if necessary. It is important to note that individuals who have experienced relapses in the past may have a personal set of warning signs that they should be attentive to.

These subjective signals may include increased anxiety, difficulty concentrating, heightened irritability, withdrawal from social activities, or changes in appetite. Maintaining self-awareness and recognizing patterns through self-reflection are crucial for early identification of relapse. Early intervention and treatment can significantly mitigate the impact of relapse, allowing individuals to regain control over their mental health and prevent the setbacks that often result from extended periods of untreated symptoms. Prompt action not only helps to minimize the severity of the relapse but also decreases the risk of potential negative consequences, such as strained relationships, difficulties in daily functioning, or suicidal thoughts. Consequently, developing a comprehensive relapse prevention plan that includes strategies for identifying early warning signs is highly recommended. This plan should involve healthcare providers, friends, and family members who can provide support, intervene when necessary, and facilitate access to professional help. By proactively recognizing the signs of relapse, individuals can work towards maintaining stability in their mental health, fostering healthy relationships, and successfully readjusting to the demands of everyday life after the holiday season.

SEEKING HELP

Encouraging individuals to reach out to mental health professionals ensures adequate support and proper management of depressive symptoms. Depression is a serious mental health disorder that can have a profound impact on an individual's daily life, relationships, and overall well-being. It is crucial for those experiencing depressive symptoms to seek help from mental health professionals to ensure they have access to the appropriate support and resources needed for effective management and treatment. Mental health professionals, such as therapists and counselors, are trained to assess and diagnose depression, as well as provide evidence-based treatments and interventions. These professionals can offer a safe and supportive environment for individuals to explore their emotions, thoughts, and behaviors, and work collaboratively to develop personalized treatment plans. Seeking help from mental health professionals can also help individuals gain a better understanding of their symptoms, and the underlying causes and triggers of their depression. This can be particularly beneficial in identifying any external factors, such as relationship problems or work-related stressors, that may be exacerbating depressive symptoms. Mental health professionals can provide individuals with the necessary tools and coping strategies to manage these challenges, and develop healthier ways of dealing with stress and negative emotions. Mental health professionals can monitor and assess individuals for any potential risks, such as thoughts of self-harm or suicide, and provide immediate interventions and referrals if needed. This ensures that individuals receive the necessary support and interventions to prevent any further deterioration of their mental health. Mental health professionals can also collaborate with other healthcare providers, such as primary care physicians or psychiatrists, to develop comprehensive treatment plans that incorporate medication management if necessary. This multi-disciplinary approach ensures that individuals receive holistic and well-rounded care, addressing both the psychological and physiological aspects of their depression. It is important to recognize that seeking help from mental health professionals is not a sign of weakness or failure, but rather a proactive and empowering step towards better mental health. By encouraging individuals to reach out to mental health professionals, we can help break down the barriers and stigma associated with seeking help for depression. It is crucial to cultivate a supportive and non-judgmental environment where individuals feel comfortable discussing their mental health concerns and seeking assistance. By doing so, we can ensure that individuals receive the adequate support and resources needed to effectively manage and overcome depressive symptoms, and ultimately improve their overall well-being and quality of life. During the holiday season, individuals often experience a break from their regular routines, which can lead to a sense of disorientation and adjustment upon returning to normal life. This period of readjustment can have a significant impact on the emotional well-being and relationships of individuals, potentially triggering feelings of depression. The abrupt transition from a festive and joyful environment filled with love and togetherness to the mundane and sometimes monotonous routine of everyday life can be difficult to navigate. This can be especially true for individuals who struggle with mental health issues, as the post-holiday period can exacerbate feelings of loneliness and isolation. The stark contrast between the high energy and excitement of the holiday season and the ordinary daily grind can create a sense of emptiness and longing for the past. The pressure to present a positive and cheerful demeanor during the holiday season can lead individuals to suppress their true emotions, which may resurface once the festivities come to an end. The return to routine can also impact relationships, as the focus shifts from shared holiday activities to individual re-sponsibilities and obligations. Couples who were able to spend ample time together during the holidays may find it challenging to reconnect and readjust to their usual schedules. This read-justment can be particularly difficult for couples in long-distance relationships or those where one or both partners have demanding work or school commitments. The reintegration into daily life can often lead to a decrease in quality time spent with loved ones, which may leave couples feeling disconnected and distant from one another. In order to navigate this post-holiday transition with minimal negative impact, it is essential for indi-viduals to prioritize self-care and open communication. Engag-ing in activities that promote mental well-being, such as exer-cise, journaling, or seeking therapy, can help individuals man-age their post-holiday depression and alleviate feelings of emp-tiness. It is vital for individuals to communicate with their loved ones about their emotions and experiences during this period. This open dialogue can foster understanding and empathy, helping couples and families navigate the readjustment process together. By prioritizing self-care and maintaining open lines of communication, individuals can mitigate the negative effects of the post-holiday blues and strengthen their relationships.

The return to routine after the holiday season can present challenges for individuals' mental well-being and relationships. The abrupt transition from a festive and joyful atmosphere to the daily grind can trigger feelings of depression and a sense of longing for the past. Couples may struggle to reconnect and readjust to their usual schedules, potentially leading to feelings of disconnection. By prioritizing self-care and open communication, individuals can manage their post-holiday depression and strengthen their relationships, mitigating the negative effects of this readjustment period.

VI. COMMUNICATION CHALLENGES

Communication can often be a challenge in any relationship, and the post-holiday period is no exception.

After all the busyness and excitement of the holidays, individuals may find it difficult to transition back to their regular routines. With the pressure to meet expectations and maintain a semblance of harmony, partners may struggle to effectively communicate their needs and emotions. This can lead to misunderstandings, tension, and increased feelings of isolation. The post-holiday period can bring about a variety of emotions, including sadness, anxiety, and exhaustion, which can further hinder effective communication. Partners may be experiencing the post-holiday blues or trying to navigate newfound stressors, such as financial strain or increased work pressures. These emotions can act as barriers to open and honest communication, making it harder to address issues and find resolutions.

Similarly, the post-holiday period may also present new challenges to long-distance relationships. After spending quality time together during the holidays, partners may now find themselves physically separated once again. This can be especially difficult as the routine sets in, and the sense of loneliness and longing for one another grows. Distance can strain communication even further, as partners may rely heavily on technology to maintain contact, which can sometimes lead to misinterpretation or a sense of disconnectedness. For individuals experiencing depression, communication challenges can become even more pronounced during this time. Depression can make it difficult to express oneself, articulate feelings, or engage in meaningful conversation. Loved ones may not fully understand the depth of their partner's emotional state, further complicating effective communication. It is essential for partners to be patient and understanding, and to seek professional help if needed, to address and manage the challenges they face. In order to overcome communication hurdles, it is crucial for partners to prioritize active listening, empathy, and validation. Taking the time to truly understand and validate each other's feelings can create a supportive environment where open communication can thrive. Couples may benefit from setting aside specific time each day to talk and check in with each other, allowing for a consistent and structured space for conversation. Recognizing the unique communication challenges that arise during the post-holiday period is essential for maintaining a strong and healthy relationship. By acknowledging and addressing these challenges head-on, partners can work together to navigate the transition and ensure a positive and fulfilling post-holiday experience.

FAMILY DYNAMICS

Extended periods of constant communication during the holidays can lead to emotional fatigue and strained family relationships. Extended periods of constant communication during the holidays can lead to emotional fatigue and strained family relationships. While the holiday season is often portrayed as a time of joy and togetherness, the reality is that extended periods of constant interaction with family members can be emotionally draining. The pressure to maintain a cheerful and harmonious atmosphere during this time can exacerbate existing tensions and conflicts within the family dynamic. The close proximity and constant interaction can lead to a lack of personal space and individual autonomy, further contributing to emotional fatigue. As family members spend more time together, they may find themselves feeling overwhelmed and exhausted, leading to a depletion of emotional energy. This can manifest in various ways, such as irritability, impatience, and a decreased ability to cope with stress. The strain on familial relationships can be attributed to the heightened expectations and pressures that come with the holiday season. Society often places a significant emphasis on the importance of familial bonds and the idea of a picture-perfect family gathering. This can create unrealistic expectations for individuals and families, putting an enormous amount of pressure on them to fulfill these ideals. When these expectations are not met, it can lead to disappointment, frustration, and even resentment among family members. Unresolved conflicts and past grievances may resurface during the holiday season, as family members are forced to spend extended periods of time together. The emotional fatigue that arises from constant communication can intensify these conflicts, making them more difficult to resolve and potentially causing further strain on relationships. In addition to the emotional fatigue experienced during the holiday season, the transition back to routine after the festivities can also present challenges for individuals and families. The abrupt shift from a period of relaxation, celebration, and indulgence to the demands of everyday life can be jarring and disorienting. This readjustment can lead to feelings of sadness, overwhelm, and even a sense of loss. Individuals may find it difficult to mentally and emotionally adapt to the responsibilities and pressures of work or school after a period of extended relaxation and leisure. The readjustment to a more structured routine can highlight any unresolved issues within the family dynamic, as the demands of everyday life leave less time and energy for addressing these underlying conflicts. Extended periods of constant communication during the holidays can lead to emotional fatigue and strained family relationships. The pressure to maintain a harmonious atmosphere, heightened expectations, and the lack of personal space can all contribute to this emotional fatigue. The transition back to routine after the holidays can further exacerbate these challenges, amplifying feelings of sadness and overwhelm. It is important for individuals and families to recognize these potential difficulties and take steps to prioritize self-care and open communication in order to maintain healthy relationships and successfully navigate the post-holiday period.

ACTIVE LISTENING

Practicing active listening and empathy can mend and strengthen family bonds. During the holiday season, many individuals experience heightened levels of stress and, as a result, their relationships may become strained. Whether it be due to financial burdens, overwhelming social obligations, or simply the pressure to create a perfect experience for loved ones, the holiday season can take a toll on one's mental and emotional well-being. By actively listening to one another and demonstrating empathy, families can begin the healing process and build stronger connections. Active listening involves fully engaging in a conversation, not just hearing the words being spoken but also placing yourself in the speaker's shoes. It requires undivided attention and a genuine interest in understanding the other person's perspective. By actively listening, family members can create a safe and supportive environment where everyone feels heard and validated. Active listening can help prevent misunderstandings and conflicts by ensuring that all parties involved are on the same page. Empathy goes hand in hand with active listening and plays a vital role in repairing strained family bonds. It involves recognizing and understanding the emotions and experiences of others, even if they differ from our own. During the post-holiday readjustment period, individuals may be feeling particularly vulnerable or sensitive. Showing empathy towards one another's struggles and acknowledging their emotions can foster a deeper sense of closeness and trust. It lets the other person know that their feelings are valid and that they are not alone in their struggles. Family members can practice empathy by actively seeking to understand each other's perspectives, validating each other's feelings, and offering support and reassurance. By actively listening and demonstrating empathy, families can mend and strengthen their bonds after the holiday season. This process acknowledges the challenges individuals face during this time and aims to create a more compassionate and understanding environment. It allows family members to reconnect on a deeper level and rebuild the trust and harmony that may have been compromised. Active listening and empathy can serve as valuable tools beyond the holiday season. By fostering open and empathetic communication, families can establish healthier patterns of interaction that will benefit them in the long run. Practicing active listening and empathy is essential for the healing and strengthening of family bonds following the holiday season. It requires genuine engagement, an eagerness to understand one another, and a willingness to validate and support each other's experiences. Through active listening and empathy, families can create a safe and compassionate environment where everyone feels heard, understood, and valued. This process allows for the resolution of conflicts, the prevention of misunderstandings, and the cultivation of stronger and more resilient relationships.

SETTING BOUNDARIES

Establishing clear boundaries with family members promotes healthy communication and minimizes conflicts.

As the holiday season comes to an end and individuals return to their daily routines, it becomes crucial to address the importance of setting boundaries with family members. Without clear guidelines, relationships can become strained, leading to misunderstandings and conflicts. Setting boundaries allows individuals to communicate their needs and expectations effectively, creating a more harmonious environment. By establishing boundaries, individuals are able to maintain their identity and independence while still maintaining strong family ties. When boundaries are not set, the lines of communication blur, making it difficult for family members to understand each other's limits and desires. This can lead to emotional fatigue, resentment, and Damaged relationships. By clearly defining personal boundaries, family members can navigate their interactions with respect and understanding, ensuring healthy communication. For example, an individual may communicate that they need some alone time after a long day of work or may emphasize the importance of privacy in certain situations. These boundaries promote personal well-being by allowing an individual to recharge and maintain a sense of individuality amidst family dynamics. Boundaries aid in resolving conflicts by providing a foundation for open and honest communication. When individuals are aware of each other's boundaries, they are less likely to overstep them, leading to a more peaceful and respectful exchange of ideas. Boundaries also enable family members to express themselves without fear of judgment or rejection, fostering a nurturing environment for open discussions. Setting boundaries within a family demonstrates a level of mutual respect and understanding. Each family member has unique needs and aspirations that should be acknowledged and respected for healthy relationships to flourish. By establishing clear boundaries, individuals can validate their own desires while promoting empathy and acceptance within the family unit. It is important to note that setting boundaries requires on-going communication and adjustment. As individuals grow and change, so do their boundaries. Thus, it becomes crucial for family members to engage in continuous dialogue and re-evaluate their limits to ensure they align with one another's needs. Establishing clear boundaries with family members is vital in promoting healthy communication and minimizing conflicts. By clearly defining personal limits, individuals can maintain their sense of self while fostering strong family ties. Boundaries facilitate respectful interactions, aid in conflict resolution, and contribute to personal well-being. Ongoing dialogue and flexibility are essential to ensure that boundaries remain effective and in line with each family member's evolving needs.

The holiday season often brings about a sense of melancholy and depression for many individuals, and readjusting to the routine after this time can prove to be quite challenging. This is because the holidays are typically associated with feelings of joy and togetherness, and when they come to an end, it can leave individuals feeling empty and disconnected. Research has shown that the post-holiday period is marked by an increase in symptoms of depression, as individuals struggle to return to their daily lives and find meaning in the mundane tasks and responsibilities. The contrast between the exciting and festive atmosphere of the holidays and the regular routine can be especially difficult for those who already struggle with mental health issues. For people with depression, the holidays can serve as a temporary escape from their usual challenges, and the return to routine can exacerbate their feelings of sadness and hopelessness. The holiday season's emphasis on family and close relationships can further contribute to feelings of loneliness and isolation once it ends. Families and friends may have spent an extended period together, creating memories and strengthening bonds; Returning to their separate lives can make individuals feel disconnected and without the social support they have had during the holidays. This sense of loss and loneliness can be particularly devastating and can amplify preexisting struggles with depression. Readjusting to the routine after the holidays can also be challenging due to the pressures and expectations that come with it. Many people may feel overwhelmed by the demands of work or school after enjoying leisurely days during the holiday break. The sudden shift from relaxation and indulgence to responsibilities and deadlines can be jarring and contribute to feelings of stress and anxiety. Individuals may feel pressure to achieve New Year's resolutions and make positive changes in their lives, adding to the strain of readjustment. The post-holiday period can be a difficult time for many individuals as they attempt to re-enter their regular routine. The contrast between the joyous holiday season and the mundane everyday life can trigger feelings of depression and loneliness. The loss of social connections and the pressures of readjustment can compound these struggles, making it essential for individuals to prioritize self-care and seek support during this time. By recognizing the challenges posed by this period and taking proactive steps to manage them, individuals can mitigate the impact of post-holiday blues and find a sense of fulfillment and well-being in their daily lives.

VII. RETURN TO WORK OR SCHOOL

Returning to work or school after the holiday season can be both a relief and a challenge. On one hand, it signifies a return to routine and structure, which can be comforting for those who thrive on consistency. It provides a sense of purpose and accomplishment as individuals delve back into their professional or educational responsibilities. The return to work or school can offer a respite from the potential stress and tension that may have plagued holiday interactions or family dynamics. This can be especially beneficial for those who experienced depressive symptoms during the holiday season, as the focus on work or school can shift their attention away from negative emotions or troubled relationships. The return to work or school can also be a daunting experience for individuals struggling with depression or relationship difficulties. The transition from a relaxed and festive atmosphere to a demanding and structured environment can be overwhelming, exacerbating feelings of sadness and anxiety. The pressure to perform at a high level academically or professionally can become a source of stress, further intensifying depressive symptoms. Negative experiences during the holiday season, such as conflicts with family members or strained relationships, may carry over into the work or school setting, making it difficult for individuals to fully engage or find solace in their daily activities. For those experiencing depression or relationship issues, the return to work or school can be an opportunity for growth and improvement. It allows individuals to establish a support network outside of their immediate family, whether it be through friendships with colleagues or connections with classmates. Engaging in work or school-related activities can foster a sense of accomplishment and self-worth, providing a much-needed boost to one's mental well-being. The structured nature of these environments can also provide individuals with a sense of purpose and direction, allowing them to regain a sense of control over their lives. To facilitate a successful transition back to work or school, individuals can employ various strategies. It is crucial to prioritize self-care and establish healthy coping mechanisms to manage stress and prevent depressive symptoms from worsening. This may involve engaging in physical exercise, practicing mindfulness or relaxation techniques, or seeking professional help through therapy or counseling. Establishing a support system at work or school, whether it is through joining clubs or organizations, attending networking events, or seeking guidance from mentors, can also be beneficial in overcoming any challenges faced. Maintaining a healthy work-life balance is essential to prevent burnout and maintain overall well-being. The return to work or school after the holiday season can offer both relief and challenges. While it provides structure and purpose, it can also exacerbate depressive symptoms and relationship difficulties. Nevertheless, through self-care, seeking support, and maintaining a healthy work-life balance, individuals can navigate this transition successfully and find solace in their daily activities. The return to work or school can serve as an opportunity for growth, personal development, and healing for those struggling with depression or strained relationships.

PERFORMANCE CHALLENGES

After a long break, individuals may struggle to regain focus and productivity at work or school.

One of the challenges individuals face after a long break is the difficulty of regaining focus and productivity at work or school. Taking time off during holidays or extended breaks can disrupt regular routines and create a sense of detachment from daily responsibilities. The transition from a relaxed holiday atmosphere back into a structured work or academic environment can be jarring and overwhelming. Not only do individuals have to contend with the mental and emotional readjustment, but they also have to catch up on missed work or coursework. This added pressure can make it even harder to regain focus and productivity. The post-holiday period often brings about a sense of fatigue and a lack of motivation. This can be attributed to the shift in routine and the readjustment to the demanding nature of work or school. The relaxed pace of the holidays can make it challenging for individuals to quickly adapt to the productivity and focus required in their daily lives. The break from work or school may have caused a decline in skills or knowledge, leading to feelings of incompetence and frustration. Individuals may struggle to recall information or complete tasks efficiently, which can further contribute to a decline in productivity. In addition, the abundance of distractions during the holiday season, such as social events and travel, can make it difficult for individuals to switch their mindset back to work or school mode. The presence of these distractions can disrupt a person's ability to concentrate and prioritize their responsibilities. The post-holiday period can also bring about feelings of post-holiday blues or depression, which can further hamper an individual's focus and productivity. The contrast between the joy and relaxation of the holidays and the demands of work or school can lead to a sense of dissatisfaction or disappointment. These negative emotions can affect an individual's ability to concentrate and perform effectively. To combat these performance challenges, individuals can implement strategies that ease the transition back to work or school. Creating a detailed plan or schedule can help individuals regain focus and stay organized. Breaking down tasks into smaller, manageable chunks can make them less daunting and more achievable. Setting realistic goals and prioritizing tasks can also help individuals stay on track and accomplish their responsibilities effectively. Individuals can use techniques such as time-blocking or the Pomodoro Technique to enhance their productivity. These methods involve setting specific time limits for focused work and incorporating short breaks to maintain focus and prevent burnout. Practicing self-care and managing stress levels can also contribute to improved focus and productivity. Maintaining a healthy lifestyle by getting enough sleep, eating nutritious meals, and engaging in regular physical activity can help individuals feel more energized and motivated. Preparing mentally and emotionally for the post-holiday transition by practicing relaxation techniques or seeking social support can also contribute to a smoother readjustment period. By implementing these strategies, individuals can overcome the challenges of regaining focus and productivity after a long break and transition more smoothly back into their work or school routine.

GOAL SETTING

Setting achievable goals and breaking tasks into smaller steps help individuals gradually regain their work or academic momentum. Goal setting is an essential aspect of regaining work or academic momentum after the holiday season. When individuals find themselves feeling overwhelmed or lacking motivation, setting achievable goals can help them regain focus and gradually transition back into their usual routine. By setting goals, individuals can identify the specific tasks they need to accomplish, breaking them down into smaller, manageable steps. This approach allows individuals to take gradual steps towards achieving their goals, which can help them build momentum and regain their confidence as they make progress. Breaking tasks into smaller steps also helps to alleviate feelings of being overwhelmed, as it provides a clear roadmap for what needs to be done. Setting achievable goals provides individuals with a sense of structure and direction, which can be especially beneficial after the holiday season when routines may have been disrupted. By setting achievable goals, individuals can also experience a greater sense of accomplishment as they work towards their objectives. Accomplishing smaller tasks can boost self-confidence and motivation, encouraging individuals to continue working towards their goals. In this way, goal setting serves as a powerful tool for individuals to regain their work or academic momentum after the holidays. Goal setting can also help individuals prioritize tasks and manage their time effectively. By identifying what needs to be done and breaking tasks into smaller steps, individuals can better plan and allocate their time and resources. Setting achievable goals also provides individuals with a sense of direction, enabling them to stay focused and avoid distractions. This sense of purpose can be particularly important after the holiday season, when individuals may be faced with various competing demands and responsibilities.

Setting achievable goals can also have a positive impact on individuals' mental health and well-being. Having clear goals and a sense of direction can reduce feelings of anxiety and stress, as individuals know what they need to accomplish and how to go about it. The process of setting and achieving goals can also provide individuals with a sense of control and agency over their lives, which can be empowering and contribute to enhanced mental well-being. Setting achievable goals and breaking tasks into smaller steps is a valuable strategy for individuals looking to regain their work or academic momentum after the holiday season. This approach provides structure, direction, and a sense of accomplishment, ultimately helping individuals gradually transition back into their routines. Goal setting can assist with time management, prioritization, and stress reduction, resulting in improved mental well-being. By utilizing goal setting techniques, individuals can overcome feelings of being overwhelmed and build the necessary momentum to succeed in their work or academic pursuits.

SEEKING SUPPORT

Engaging with colleagues, professors, or mentors can provide guidance and encouragement during the readjustment process. Engaging with colleagues, professors, or mentors can play a pivotal role in providing guidance and encouragement during the readjustment process. Returning to the college routine after the holiday break can often be a challenging and overwhelming experience for many students. Seeking support from those around us can greatly alleviate the stress and anxiety that often accompanies this period of transition. Colleagues who have gone through similar struggles in the past can provide valuable insights and advice on how to navigate through this phase successfully. By sharing their own experiences, they can offer practical tips and strategies that have worked for them, thereby empowering students to find their own effective coping mechanisms. Professors, on the other hand, can provide students with academic guidance and support. They can offer resources and reading materials that can help students catch up with missed coursework or assignments and provide additional guidance if needed. Professors can be a source of motivation and encouragement, assuring students that they are not alone in facing challenges and struggles related to readjustment. They can also offer valuable feedback and guidance on how to manage time effectively and balance academic and personal responsibilities. Mentors can play a crucial role by offering guidance and support through their own experiences and expertise. Their wisdom and encouragement can provide students with the reassurance that they are on the right track and that readjustment after the holidays is a common experience for many. Mentors can help students identify and navigate their strengths and weaknesses, guiding them towards personalized solutions for readjustment challenges. By seeking support from colleagues, professors, and mentors, students can receive the guidance and encouragement they need during the readjustment process. These individuals can provide invaluable insights, advice, and resources, helping students develop effective coping mechanisms to manage the stresses and anxieties that come with readjustment to the college routine. Engaging with these individuals can also instill a sense of validation and reassurance, reminding students that they are not alone in their struggles. Through these supportive relationships, students can gain the tools and confidence to overcome any obstacles that come their way, ultimately enabling them to thrive during this crucial period of readjustment.

Readjusting to the daily routine after the holiday season can be an overwhelming and challenging experience, particularly for individuals struggling with depression and managing relationships. Hectic schedules, financial strains, and the pressure to present a picture-perfect image of happiness can exacerbate feelings of loneliness and emptiness, deepening the existing depressive symptoms. Readjusting to the constant demands of work, school, and social obligations can create additional stress and negatively impact relationships. As the holiday season often allows for more time spent with loved ones, readjusting to a routine that limits these interactions can leave individuals feeling disconnected and isolated. Consequently, this can further deteriorate one's mental well-being. The pressure to conform to societal expectations and maintain the illusion of a perfect holiday experience can also lead to feelings of failure and disappointment when things inevitably fall short of these expectations. Rather than providing a much-needed break, the holidays can hence become a breeding ground for self-doubt and self-criticism, exacerbating depressive symptoms and straining relationships. The financial strain brought on by the holiday season can compound the individual's emotional burden. Gift-giving expectations and the desire to create memorable experiences often lead to overspending, placing individuals in a compromised financial position in the aftermath of the celebrations. The looming debts and bills can further fuel anxiety and depression, creating a vicious cycle of negative emotions. For individuals who are already struggling with financial difficulties, the added pressure of holiday expenses can be overwhelming and lead to a deep sense of hopelessness and despair. Consequently, this strain can significantly impact relationships, as financial stress often becomes a divisive factor between partners, friends, and family members. The return to a daily routine after the festivities can be emotionally and mentally draining, further exacerbating feelings of depression. The sudden shift from a relaxed and carefree holiday ambiance to the demands of work, school, and other responsibilities can be jarring and disorienting. The loss of freedom and leisure time can lead to a sense of entrapment, trapping individuals in a cycle of despair and resentment. This newfound stress and exhaustion can breed frustration and irritability, posing challenges for maintaining healthy and mutually supportive relationships. The strain on relationships may be particularly noticeable in those where one partner had higher expectations for the holidays than the other, leading to feelings of resentment and disappointment. Consequently, readjustment after the holidays can become a crucial period for individuals with depression, as it requires reestablishing healthy coping mechanisms and effective communication strategies with loved ones. Readjusting to routine, depression management, and maintaining healthy relationships after the holiday season can present significant challenges. The pressure to conform to societal expectations, financial strains, and the sudden shift from relaxation to the demands of daily life can exacerbate depressive symptoms and strain relationships. It is important for individuals navigating these post-holiday challenges to prioritize self-care, communicate openly with loved ones, and seek professional support if needed. By addressing these challenges proactively, individuals can find stability, self-compassion, and strengthened relationships throughout this transitional period.

VIII. FINANCIAL STRESS

Another source of stress that many individuals experience after the holidays is financial stress. The holiday season often involves increased spending on gifts, travel, and entertainment, which can leave people feeling overwhelmed by the financial burden they have accumulated. This financial stress can be especially challenging for college students who are already facing the demands of tuition fees and living expenses. The pressure to keep up with their peers and provide the perfect gifts for loved ones can lead to feelings of anxiety and inadequacy. Students may find themselves struggling to make ends meet as they try to balance their academic responsibilities with part-time jobs, leaving little time for relaxation and enjoyment. This constant financial strain can take a toll on mental health and well-being, potentially leading to feelings of hopelessness and despair. Financial stress can have a negative impact on relationships, causing tension and conflict between partners and family members. The inability to meet financial obligations and expectations can create an environment of strain and resentment, leading to a breakdown in communication and intimacy. Financial stress can cause individuals to isolate themselves from social activities, fearing judgment or feeling ashamed of their inability to participate. This isolation can further exacerbate feelings of loneliness and depression. To alleviate financial stress, it is important for individuals to establish a realistic budget and prioritize their spending. This may involve making sacrifices and setting limits on unnecessary expenses. Seeking financial advice and support from resources available on campus and within the community can also be helpful in managing debts and establishing a solid financial plan. Open and honest communication with partners and loved ones about financial struggles can reduce tension and foster a supportive environment. It is crucial to remember that material possessions do not define one's worth or happiness. Although it can be challenging to resist societal pressures, embracing the value of meaningful experiences and personal connections can provide a sense of fulfillment and reduce the burden of financial stress. By proactively addressing financial stress and seeking support, individuals can effectively manage this aspect of post-holiday readjustment and regain a sense of control and well-being in their lives.

OVERSPENDING DURING THE HOLIDAYS

Excessive spending during the festive season can lead to financial stress and anxiety post-holidays.

During the holiday season, it is not uncommon for individuals to engage in overspending. The temptation to purchase gifts for loved ones and indulge in materialistic desires often leads to excessive spending. This practice can have negative consequences, as it can result in financial stress and anxiety once the holidays are over. Overspending during the festive season can lead to a significant amount of debt, which may take months or even years to repay. This debt can weigh heavily on individuals, causing them to experience feelings of stress, anxiety, and even depression. The financial burden may also impact relationships, as individuals may struggle to fulfill their financial obligations, potentially leading to conflicts and strain within the family unit. The pressure to maintain a certain level of consumption during the holidays can create a cycle of overspending that becomes difficult to break, perpetuating the cycle of financial stress and anxiety. Once the excitement and joy of the holiday season fade away, individuals are left to face the consequences of their overspending. They may have to make sacrifices in other areas of their life, such as cutting back on daily necessities or postponing important financial goals. These sacrifices can further contribute to feelings of stress and anxiety, as individuals are forced to confront the repercussions of their actions. The financial strain can have long-lasting effects on individuals' mental well-being. It is not uncommon for individuals to experience symptoms of depression after the holidays, as they grapple with the realization of the financial burden they have accumulated. The pressure to present a happy and joyous facade during the holidays can also contribute to feelings of isolation and inadequacy, causing individuals to withdraw from their social circles and further exacerbating their depression. The financial stress and anxiety post-holidays can impact individuals' ability to readjust to their normal routines. The worry over debt and financial obligations can consume individuals' thoughts, making it difficult for them to focus and concentrate on their daily tasks. The added stress can also affect their physical health, leading to increased levels of fatigue and overall decreased well-being. In order to prevent excessive spending during the holidays and the subsequent financial stress and anxiety, it is important for individuals to establish a budget and stick to it. By setting clear boundaries on spending and prioritizing financial goals, individuals can avoid the pitfalls of overspending and maintain their financial well-being. It is crucial to communicate openly with loved ones about expectations and financial capabilities. By having honest conversations about gift-giving and budget limitations, individuals can alleviate some of the pressure to overspend and foster healthier, more meaningful connections during the holiday season.

BUDGETING AND PLANNING

Creating a realistic budget and prioritizing necessary expenses can alleviate financial strain. Once the holiday season has come to an end, many individuals find themselves facing the daunting reality of post-holiday expenses. From buying gifts for loved ones to hosting elaborate parties, the holiday season often leads to an increase in spending. Consequently, financial strain becomes a significant concern for many. By implementing effective budgeting and planning strategies, individuals can alleviate this strain and regain control over their finances.

Creating a realistic budget is the first step in managing one's finances effectively. It involves carefully assessing income and expenses and making informed decisions about spending. By identifying fixed expenses such as rent, utilities, and loan payments, individuals can determine the proportion of their income that needs to be allocated to these necessities. With this information at hand, discretionary expenses, such as entertainment and dining out, can be evaluated and adjusted accordingly. For example, opting for home-cooked meals overeating out can help reduce expenses significantly. By consciously setting spending limits and monitoring one's expenditures, individuals can ensure that they are not living beyond their means.

Prioritizing necessary expenses is another essential aspect of budgeting and planning. When facing financial strain, it is crucial to differentiate between wants and needs. This requires aligning expenses with one's priorities and focusing on the essentials. For instance, individuals may need to prioritize paying off high-interest debts or set aside funds for emergencies. By making these necessary expenses a priority, individuals can avoid accumulating more debt and establish a more stable financial situation. It may be beneficial to explore alternative options for certain expenses, such as negotiating lower interest rates or refinancing loans. By actively seeking the most cost-effective solutions, individuals can optimize their budget and decrease financial burden. Implementing effective budgeting and planning strategies not only helps to alleviate financial strain but also promotes a sense of empowerment and control over one's finances. Rather than being overwhelmed by financial obligations, individuals can take proactive steps towards achieving financial stability. By creating a realistic budget and prioritizing necessary expenses, individuals can actively manage their finances and make informed choices about spending. These strategies foster a sense of discipline and accountability, encouraging individuals to develop healthier spending habits in the long run. The post-holiday season often brings about financial strain for many individuals. By implementing effective budgeting and planning strategies, individuals can regain control over their finances and alleviate this strain. Creating a realistic budget allows individuals to assess and adjust their income and expenses accordingly. Prioritizing necessary expenses helps individuals distinguish between wants and needs, enabling them to focus resources on essential obligations. By taking these proactive steps towards financial stability, individuals can not only alleviate financial strain but also cultivate healthier spending habits for the future.

SEEKING PROFESSIONAL HELP

Financial advisors or credit counselors can offer guidance and strategies to manage post-holiday debt effectively.

Seeking professional help, such as financial advisors or credit counselors, can be an effective way to manage post-holiday debt. These professionals have the knowledge and expertise to offer guidance and strategies for individuals burdened with excessive debt after the holiday season. Financial advisors can provide valuable insights into budgeting, saving, and investing, helping individuals develop a long-term plan to pay off their debts. They can analyze a person's financial situation, evaluate their income and expenses, and recommend appropriate steps to take. Financial advisors can educate individuals about different debt consolidation options, such as debt management plans or debt consolidation loans. These options can help individuals combine their debts into a single, more manageable monthly payment, with potentially lower interest rates. Credit counselors, on the other hand, specialize in debt management and can offer personalized plans to help individuals regain control over their finances. They can negotiate with creditors to lower interest rates, waive fees, or create affordable repayment plans. Credit counselors can also provide guidance on developing a realistic budget, prioritizing debt payments, and establishing healthy financial habits. They can offer resources and educational materials, enabling individuals to strengthen their financial literacy skills and make informed decisions. Seeking the assistance of financial advisors or credit counselors can help individuals alleviate the stress and anxiety associated with post-holiday debt. These professionals create a supportive and non-judgmental environment, allowing individuals to openly discuss their financial concerns. By providing tailored solutions and strategies, financial advisors and credit counselors empower individuals to take control of their financial situation, ultimately leading to a more stable and secure future. It is important to recognize that asking for help does not signify weakness or failure but rather a proactive step towards improving one's financial well-being. Individuals should not hesitate to reach out to professionals in times of financial distress. Seeking professional help from financial advisors or credit counselors can offer valuable guidance and strategies to effectively manage post-holiday debt. These professionals bring specialized expertise and knowledge to assist individuals in developing and implementing a plan to regain control over their finances. By working with financial advisors or credit counselors, individuals can create realistic budgets, explore debt consolidation options, and establish healthy financial habits.

Seeking professional help can lead to a reduced financial burden and increased peace of mind. As the holiday season comes to an end, individuals often find themselves facing a range of emotions and challenges as they attempt to readjust to their regular routines. For some, this period can trigger feelings of depression and anxiety, making it difficult to transition back into their usual daily activities. The abrupt shift from a time filled with joy, excitement, and celebration to the monotony of everyday life can leave individuals feeling empty and lacking purpose. The holiday season often comes with a sense of togetherness, as people spend time with loved ones and engage in festivities that bring them closer together. The end of this period can lead to a sense of isolation as social gatherings cease, and people return to their usual obligations and responsibilities. This sudden change in social dynamic can be particularly challenging for individuals who heavily rely on the support and company of others to maintain their emotional well-being. Without the constant distraction and connection that the holidays provide, it becomes easier for negative thoughts and feelings to resurface, emphasizing personal dissatisfaction and feelings of emptiness. Readjusting to the regular routine after the holidays can also prove to be a challenge in maintaining healthy relationships. The holiday season often acts as a time for people to reconnect with family and friends, creating opportunities for meaningful interactions and strengthening bonds. The end of the holidays can signify a return to the daily grind, leaving less time and energy available to invest in relationships. As individuals become consumed by work, school, and other obligations, maintaining strong relationships can take a back seat, leading to feelings of neglect and resentment. The post-holiday period can affect relationships in unexpected ways, as stress levels increase due to the demands of daily life. This added pressure can result in heightened conflict, as individuals struggle to balance their own readjustment with the needs and expectations of their partners or loved ones. Navigating the transition from the holiday season back to routine often presents individuals with a myriad of challenges, both internally and externally. The sudden shift from joyous celebrations to the realities of everyday life can trigger feelings of depression and anxiety, impacting overall mental well-being. Similarly, relationships can suffer as individuals struggle to reestablish regular routines and find the time and energy to prioritize their connections. As this readjustment period poses various difficulties for individuals, it is crucial to recognize the unique challenges it presents and actively work to support one's emotional well-being and relationships through self-care practices and open communication.

IX. ESTABLISHING NEW ROUTINES

Once the holiday season comes to an end, many individuals find themselves struggling to readjust to their regular routines. This can be especially challenging for those who have been suffering from depression during this time. Establishing new routines can play a crucial role in helping individuals regain a sense of stability and control in their lives. One way to establish a new routine is by setting daily goals and creating a schedule. By taking the time to write down specific tasks and allocating time for each, individuals can create a sense of structure and purpose. This can help combat feelings of aimlessness and provide a sense of accomplishment as tasks are completed. Incorporating self-care activities into the daily routine can be highly beneficial. Engaging in activities such as exercise, meditation, or hobbies can help improve mood and overall well-being. It is important to establish a regular sleep schedule. Adequate sleep is essential for mental health and can help alleviate symptoms of depression. By going to bed and waking up at consistent times, individuals can ensure they are getting the recommended amount of sleep and improve their overall quality of rest. Another important aspect of establishing new routines is maintaining healthy relationships. The holiday season often allows for additional time spent with loved ones, but once the festivities end, it is crucial to continue nurturing these connections. Scheduling regular outings or simply setting aside time for meaningful conversations can help prevent feelings of loneliness or isolation. Seeking support from friends, family members, or mental health professionals can be incredibly beneficial. Having someone to talk to and share experiences with can provide invaluable emotional support. It is important to remain flexible and allow for adjustment periods. Transitioning from one routine to another can be difficult, and it is normal to feel overwhelmed or frustrated at times. It is crucial to remember that establishing new routines takes time, patience, and self-compassion. By acknowledging the progress already made and focusing on small, achievable goals, individuals can gradually settle into their new routines and experience improvements in their mental health and overall well-being. Establishing new routines after the holiday season can be challenging, but it is crucial in helping individuals readjust and overcome depression. By setting daily goals, incorporating self-care activities, maintaining healthy relationships, and seeking support, individuals can regain a sense of stability and control in their lives. Remaining flexible and allowing for adjustment periods is vital in successfully transitioning to a new routine. Putting effort into establishing new routines can lead to improvements in mental health and overall well-being.

EMBRACING CHANGE

The post-holiday period can serve as an opportunity to establish new, healthier routines. In the aftermath of the holiday season, individuals often feel a pang of sadness and disorientation as they say goodbye to the festivities and return to their daily routines. This post-holiday period also provides a unique opportunity to embrace change and establish new, healthier routines. As the decorations are boxed away and the last remnants of holiday indulgence are consumed, it becomes apparent that a reset is needed. This transitional phase allows individuals to reflect on their habits and make conscious efforts to improve their overall well-being. For instance, one may choose to incorporate regular exercise into their daily schedule, incorporating a morning jog or an evening yoga session. This small change can lead to significant improvements in both physical and mental health, not to mention the potential for weight management and increased energy levels. The post-holiday period offers a chance to reevaluate dietary choices. Instead of relying on rich holiday leftovers and excessive sweets, individuals can focus on nourishing their bodies with whole foods and balanced meals. This shift can lead to improved digestion, increased nutrient intake, and an overall enhanced mood. This transitional period allows individuals to refocus on their personal goals and aspirations. Whether it is pursuing a new hobby, enrolling in a class, or taking steps towards career advancement, this time presents an opportunity to prioritize personal growth and self-improvement. The post-holiday period fosters a spirit of renewal and reinvention. It is a time to declutter both physically and mentally, eliminating unnecessary possessions and toxic relationships. This allows individuals to create space for new opportunities and positive experiences. By shedding the weight of the past, whether it is in the form of material possessions or negative emotions, individuals can lay the groundwork for a brighter and more fulfilling future. While the post-holiday period may evoke feelings of sadness and disorientation, it also presents an opportunity for growth and positive change. By embracing the need for a reset and establishing new, healthier routines, individuals can improve their physical and mental well-being. Whether it is through adopting a regular exercise regimen, reevaluating dietary choices, pursuing personal goals, or decluttering their lives, the post-holiday period serves as a stepping-stone towards a brighter and more fulfilling future. So, instead of succumbing to the post-holiday blues, let us seize this transitional phase as an opportunity for self-improvement and embrace the potential for positive change.

SELF-REFLECTION

Reflecting on the previous year's challenges and successes enables individuals to identify areas for personal growth and improvement. Self-reflection is a valuable tool for individuals as it allows them to evaluate and analyze their previous year's challenges and successes. By taking the time to reflect on their experiences, individuals can gain insight into their own strengths and weaknesses, as well as identify areas for personal growth and improvement. This process of self-reflection is especially important after the holidays, as this time of year can often bring about feelings of depression, strain on relationships, and the need for readjustment. The holiday season is often filled with high expectations and demands, which can be overwhelming and draining. This can lead to increased stress, anxiety, and feelings of depression. By reflecting on these challenges, individuals can better understand the factors that contributed to their emotional well-being during this time and develop strategies for managing these stressors in the future. Self-reflection allows individuals to assess the state of their relationships. The holidays can be a challenging time for relationships, as they often involve increased social interactions and expectations. Reflecting on these experiences can provide individuals with insight into the dynamics of their relationships and identify areas for improvement. By acknowledging the challenges faced during this time, individuals can work towards cultivating healthier and more fulfilling connections with others. Self-reflection after the holidays allows individuals to assess their overall adjustment to the end of this festive period. The post-holiday period can often be accompanied by a sense of let-down or emptiness, as individuals transition back to their regular routines and responsibilities. By reflecting on this readjustment process, individuals can gain a better understanding of their emotional and psychological needs during this time. They can develop strategies for managing these feelings, such as seeking support from loved ones or engaging in self-care activities. Self-reflection can help individuals set goals for personal growth. By evaluating their previous year's challenges and successes, individuals can identify areas in which they would like to improve. This could be in the form of developing new skills or habits, pursuing new interests or hobbies, or working towards personal development. Through self-reflection, individuals can chart a path for their continued growth and improvement. Self-reflection plays a crucial role in helping individuals identify areas for personal growth and improvement. By reflecting on the challenges and successes of the previous year, individuals can gain valuable insights into themselves, their relationships, and their overall well-being. This process is particularly important after the holiday season, as it allows individuals to address the unique challenges and emotions experienced during this time. Through self-reflection, individuals can discover opportunities for personal growth and set goals for their continued development.

IMPLEMENTING NEW HABITS

Gradually incorporating new habits, such as exercise or Mindfulness practices, into daily routines aids in maintaining overall well-being. Implementing new habits is a crucial aspect of maintaining overall well-being, particularly following the holiday season. Gradually incorporating new habits, such as exercise or Mindfulness practices, into daily routines can have significant benefits for both physical and mental health. Regular exercise has been shown to improve mood and reduce symptoms of depression, which may be particularly important after the often-stressful holiday season. Engaging in physical activity increases the release of endorphins, neurotransmitters in the brain that are known to elevate mood and reduce feelings of stress and anxiety. By incorporating exercise into one's daily routine, individuals can establish a consistent exercise regimen, leading to long-term improvements in both physical and mental well-being. Similarly, incorporating Mindfulness practices into daily routines can have profound effects on mental health.

Mindfulness involves bringing one's attention to the present moment, without judgment or attachment to thoughts or emotions. It has been linked to reduced stress and anxiety, and increased feelings of calm and well-being. By gradually incorporating Mindfulness exercises, such as meditation or deep breathing, into daily routines, individuals can experience the benefits of increased self-awareness and the ability to respond to stressors in a more proactive and calm manner. The gradual incorporation of new habits allows for a more sustainable approach to behavior change. When individuals attempt to make drastic changes to their routines all at once, they often become overwhelmed and discouraged, leading to a relapse into old habits. By gradually incorporating small changes into daily routines, individuals can build upon their successes over time, increasing the likelihood of long-term adherence. This approach to habit formation also allows individuals to learn and adapt as they go, making adjustments as needed to find what works best for them. Implementing new habits into daily routines is essential for maintaining overall well-being, particularly following the holiday season. Gradually incorporating habits such as exercise or Mindfulness practices can have significant benefits for both physical and mental health. By establishing a consistent exercise regimen and engaging in Mindfulness practices, individuals can improve mood, reduce stress and anxiety, and increase self-awareness. The gradual approach to habit formation allows for sustainable behavior change and increased long-term adherence. By making small changes over time and learning from their experiences, individuals can find what works best for them, leading to improved well-being and a greater sense of overall satisfaction in life. One of the significant challenges individuals face after the holiday season is readjusting back to their daily routines. The transition from the joyous and relaxed atmosphere of the holidays to the normal hustle and bustle of everyday life can be difficult for many people, particularly for those struggling with depression. This emotional condition, characterized by persistent feelings of sadness, hopelessness, and a lack of interest in previously enjoyed activities, can be exacerbated during the post-holiday period. The abrupt end of festivities can feel overwhelming and intensify existing feelings of isolation and despair. Maintaining healthy relationships can also be a struggle during this time. The holiday season often brings people together, providing an opportunity for individuals to reconnect with family and friends. As the holidays come to an end, these social connections may once again fade away. The withdrawal from the warmth and support provided by loved ones during this time can heighten feelings of loneliness and isolation, making it harder for individuals to cope with their depression. The pressure to maintain resolutions and make positive changes can add further stress and strain on relationships, leading to conflicts and difficulties in communication.

In order to combat the negative impact of readjustment after the holidays, it is essential for individuals to prioritize self-care and engage in activities that promote well-being. This can include engaging in regular exercise, maintaining a balanced diet, and getting a sufficient amount of sleep. Engaging in these self-care practices can help regulate mood and alleviate symptoms of depression. Seeking professional help and talking to a therapist or counselor can provide individuals with the necessary support and guidance to navigate through this challenging period. It is crucial for individuals to actively work on maintaining relationships and fostering social connections, even after the holidays have ended. This can involve setting aside time to engage in meaningful interactions with loved ones, maintaining regular communication, and seeking opportunities for socialization, such as joining clubs or organizations. By making a conscious effort to preserve and strengthen relationships, individuals can combat feelings of loneliness and isolation, creating a support network that is vital for their mental well-being.

Readjusting back to routine after the holidays can be a daunting task, particularly for individuals struggling with depression.

The sudden end of festivities and the resumption of normal daily life can intensify feelings of loneliness and exacerbate symptoms of depression. By prioritizing self-care, seeking professional help, and actively maintaining relationships, individuals can diminish the negative impact of readjustment, fostering a sense of stability, support, and well-being during this challenging period.

X. SOCIAL SUPPORT

Social support is a critical factor in helping individuals cope with depression, relationships, and readjustment after the holidays. During the holiday season, many people experience heightened emotions, both positive and negative, which can lead to a rollercoaster of feelings once the festivities are over. Research has consistently shown that having a strong support network can significantly contribute to one's mental well-being and overall adjustment to post-holiday life. Social support can come from various sources, including family, friends, and even online communities. These supportive relationships act as a buffer against stress and can provide individuals with the emotional, informational, and instrumental assistance they need to navigate the challenges they may face after the holiday season. Depression is a common psychological response that many individuals experience after the holiday season. The return to routine can seem mundane and lack the excitement and social engagement of the festivities. Having social support can help individuals combat these feelings of depression by offering a sense of belonging and connection. Friends and family can provide emotional support by listening and offering encouragement. They can also provide companionship and engage in activities that bring joy and fulfillment. By having individuals who understand their struggles and can provide comfort, individuals are more likely to feel less isolated and more motivated to engage in activities that promote mental well-being.

Relationships can also be significantly affected after the holiday season. The stress of the holidays, coupled with increased expectations and demands, can strain even the strongest of relationships. Having social support during this time is crucial in maintaining healthy connections and resolving conflicts. Friends and family can offer a fresh perspective, support in communication, and provide guidance in navigating difficult situations. By having a trusted support system, individuals can address relationship challenges more effectively, fostering understanding and enhancing the overall quality of their relationships.

Readjustment after the holidays can be particularly challenging as individuals transition from a period of indulgence and relaxation back to the demands of everyday life. Social support plays a key role in this process, providing individuals with the necessary resources and guidance to make a smooth and successful transition. Friends and family can offer practical assistance, such as helping with organizing and planning, managing time and priorities, and providing motivation and accountability. Being part of a supportive community, whether online or offline, can offer individuals the opportunity to share experiences, seek advice, and exchange tips on readjustment strategies.

Social support is a critical component in helping individuals cope with depression, relationships, and readjustment after the holidays. It provides individuals with the emotional, informational, and instrumental resources necessary to navigate the challenges that often arise during this time. By having a strong support network, individuals are more likely to experience improved mental well-being, enhanced relationship quality, and successful readjustment into everyday life.

IMPORTANCE OF SOCIAL CONNECTIONS

Connecting with friends, support groups, or community organizations helps combat feelings of loneliness or isolation. The importance of social connections cannot be understated when it comes to combating feelings of loneliness or isolation. Connecting with friends, support groups, or community organizations is a vital aspect of maintaining mental and emotional well-being. During the holiday season, individuals often experience a heightened sense of loneliness or isolation, as the emphasis on family and social gatherings can intensify feelings of loss or disconnection. By reaching out and engaging in social activities, individuals can find solace and support in the company of others. Friends provide a valuable network of emotional support, offering a listening ear, advice, and companionship. These connections are particularly crucial for those experiencing symptoms of depression, as social isolation is a common contributing factor. Support groups also play a vital role in combating feelings of loneliness, as they provide a safe space to share experiences, receive validation, and build connections with others who may be going through similar challenges. The act of connecting with others who understand can be incredibly therapeutic, helping individuals feel less alone in their struggles. Community organizations offer yet another avenue for social connections. Volunteering or participating in community events not only allows individuals to make a positive impact but also fosters a sense of belonging and connection. By engaging with others in such settings, individuals are exposed to diverse perspectives and experiences, expanding their social networks and enriching their lives. Beyond combating loneliness, social connections have a profound impact on overall well-being. Numerous studies have demonstrated that strong social connections positively affect physical health, mental health, and longevity. Social interactions release oxytocin, a hormone that promotes feelings of trust and bonding, which in turn reduces stress levels and boosts emotional well-being. Social connections provide a sense of purpose, as individuals feel a sense of responsibility and commitment towards maintaining these relationships. This purposeful engagement fosters resilience and facilitates coping with life's challenges. Social connections are of utmost importance, especially when combating feelings of loneliness or isolation. Friends, support groups, and community organizations all play a crucial role in fostering a sense of belonging, support, and well-being. By reaching out and actively engaging in social activities, individuals can diminish feelings of loneliness or despair while simultaneously experiencing the positive effects of meaningful connections. As individuals transition back to their routine after the holidays, prioritizing and nurturing these social connections can have a profound impact on mental and emotional health.

MAKING PLANS

Planning social activities and spending quality time with loved ones create opportunities for positive interactions.

After the holiday season, when many individuals may have experienced feelings of loneliness or depression, it becomes crucial to focus on creating opportunities for positive interactions through making plans with loved ones. Social activities and spending quality time with family and friends can significantly impact one's mental and emotional well-being. These activities allow individuals to feel a sense of belonging, build connections, and combat feelings of isolation or sadness that may arise after the holiday season. Planning social activities can range from organizing small gatherings or outings to engaging in activities such as dining out, going to movies or concerts, or participating in recreational activities. These activities provide an avenue for individuals to engage with others and strengthen their relationships. By spending quality time with loved ones, individuals can create lasting memories and foster deeper connections. Quality time can be in the form of engaging in meaningful conversations, participating in shared hobbies or interests, or simply enjoying each other's company. In addition to providing opportunities for positive interactions, planning social activities and spending quality time with loved ones also helps individuals to maintain a healthy work-life balance. The post-holiday period can often be overwhelming, as individuals readjust to their daily routines and responsibilities. By intentionally setting aside time for social engagements and loved ones, individuals can alleviate stress and prioritize personal well-being. This balance not only improves mental and emotional health but also enhances overall productivity and satisfaction in other areas of life.

Planning and engaging in social activities can also contribute to personal growth and development. When individuals engage in social interactions, they are exposed to diverse perspectives, ideas, and experiences. This exposure broadens their horizons, fosters empathy, and promotes personal growth. Social activities can serve as a platform for individuals to learn from one another, challenge their own beliefs, and acquire new skills or knowledge. By actively seeking out social connections and engaging in social activities, individuals can expand their network, develop their social skills, and cultivate a sense of community.

Making plans and engaging in social activities and spending quality time with loved ones are essential for creating opportunities for positive interactions in the post-holiday period. These activities not only combat feelings of loneliness or depression but also enhance mental and emotional well-being. By prioritizing social engagements and loved ones, individuals can maintain a healthy work-life balance, foster deeper connections, and promote personal growth and development. Thus, it is essential to recognize the significance of planning social activities and spending quality time with loved ones in order to navigate the post-holiday period successfully.

OPEN COMMUNICATION

Sharing feelings and experiences with trusted individuals fosters emotional support and encourages a sense of belonging.

Open communication is a crucial aspect of maintaining emotional well-being and a sense of belonging. The ability to share our feelings and experiences with trusted individuals provides us with emotional support and validates our experiences. When we communicate openly with others, we are able to express our thoughts and emotions, which can help alleviate stress and anxieties. Having someone to confide in and share our experiences with can provide a sense of comfort and reassurance, knowing that we are not alone in our struggles. In addition, open communication fosters a sense of belonging. When we are able to share our experiences with others, we are able to connect on a deeper level and develop a strong sense of community. This sense of belonging is vital for our emotional well-being, as it provides us with a support system through which we can navigate life's challenges. Whether it is discussing our day at work or opening up about a difficult situation, sharing our feelings and experiences with trusted individuals allows us to feel heard and understood. This, in turn, can boost our self-esteem and confidence, knowing that our experiences and perspectives are valued by others. Open communication can encourage personal growth and self-reflection. When we share our feelings and experiences, we often gain new insights and perspectives from others. This exchange of ideas and perspectives can broaden our understanding of ourselves and the world around us. By engaging in open and honest conversations, we are able to gain new insights, challenge our beliefs, and foster personal growth. Open communication can lead to strengthened relationships. When we open up and share our feelings and experiences with others, we are able to establish a deeper level of trust and intimacy. This can strengthen our relationships and help us build a strong support system. Sharing our experiences allows others to gain a better understanding of our emotional state and allows them to offer support when needed. Open communication is a powerful tool that can promote emotional well-being, foster a sense of belonging, encourage personal growth, and strengthen relationships. By developing the ability to openly communicate with trusted individuals, we can navigate life's challenges more effectively, knowing that we have the support and understanding of others. Coming back into the normal routine after the holidays can often bring about feelings of depression and anxiety. For many, the holiday season is a time of joy and togetherness, filled with festivities and celebrations. As the holiday season ends, individuals may find themselves facing a sense of sadness and longing for the special moments they experienced during this time. This post-holiday depression can be particularly challenging in the context of relationships. The holidays often provide an opportunity to reconnect with family and friends, creating a sense of belonging and support. After the holidays, the return to a normal routine can feel isolating and lonely, especially for those who tend to rely on the support of others during difficult times. Readjusting to the demands of work or school after a period of relaxation and leisure can be overwhelming, exacerbating feelings of depression. The abrupt transition from the holiday spirit to the pressures of everyday life can contribute to a sense of post-holiday letdown.

The comparison between the joyous holiday season and the mundane responsibilities of daily life can make the latter seem even more unfulfilling, leading to a decrease in overall life satisfaction. As a result, individuals may begin to question the purpose and meaning behind their daily routines, further intensifying feelings of depression and dissatisfaction. Coping with post-holiday depression and readjustment after the holidays requires a multifaceted approach. It is essential to allow oneself time to grieve the end of the holiday season and to recognize that it is normal to experience feelings of sadness during this time. Engaging in self-care activities, such as exercise, spending time outdoors, or engaging in hobbies, can help alleviate symptoms of depression and provide a sense of purpose. Seeking social support from loved ones or joining support groups can help combat feelings of isolation and loneliness. It is also important to remind oneself that a sense of purpose and joy can be found within the routines of daily life. By setting realistic goals and finding meaning in small accomplishments, individuals can regain a sense of control and satisfaction. It is crucial to maintain a balanced lifestyle, incorporating relaxation and leisure activities into daily routines, in order to mitigate the effects of post-holiday depression. Readjusting to the normal routine after the holidays can be a challenging experience, particularly in regard to depression, relationships, and overall life satisfaction. By acknowledging and addressing these difficulties through self-care, social support, and finding meaning in daily routines, individuals can effectively navigate the post-holiday period and promote their overall well-being.

XI. REKINDLING RELATIONSHIPS

After the hustle and bustle of the holiday season, the return to routine can often leave us feeling disconnected from our loved ones. It is at this time, That we must focus our efforts on rekindling our relationships and rebuilding the bonds that may have become strained during this busy period. One way to achieve this is by carving out quality time for our partners, family members, and friends. This can be done through regular date nights with our significant others or setting aside dedicated hours for catching up with loved ones over a cup of coffee. We must make a conscious effort to engage in activities that promote shared experiences and memories, such as going on hikes, cooking together, or attending social events. These shared experiences not only nurture our relationships but also provide an opportunity for growth and exploration as a couple or group. Communication is also crucial in reigniting relationships that may have been neglected during the holiday chaos. We must be willing to listen attentively to our loved ones, understanding their needs, desires, and concerns. In doing so, we demonstrate empathy and show that we value and respect their feelings. It is essential to express our gratitude and affection towards our loved ones regularly. Simple acts of kindness, such as saying "thank you" or giving compliments, can go a long way in fostering emotional connection. By expressing our love and appreciation, we nourish the emotional bonds that hold our relationships together. It is important to acknowledge and address any conflicts or unresolved issues that may have arisen during the holiday season. Honesty, compassion, and a willingness to compromise are key to resolving conflicts and moving forward together. We must approach these conversations with an open mind and a genuine desire to find a solution that satisfies all parties involved. Self-care plays a vital role in rekindling relationships. Taking care of our mental, emotional, and physical well-being not only allows us to show up fully in our relationships but also encourages our loved ones to do the same. Engaging in activities we enjoy, seeking support when needed, and maintaining a healthy work-life balance all contribute to a happier and more fulfilling life, which in turn strengthens our relationships. While the return to routine after the holidays can be challenging, it is also an opportunity for us to rekindle our relationships. By making time for our loved ones, communication, expressing gratitude, addressing conflicts, and practicing self-care, we can rebuild and strengthen the connections that sustain us. So let us embrace this chance to grow closer, creating a thriving support network that will carry us through the challenges and joys of everyday life.

RELATIONSHIP REJUVENATION

The post-holiday period provides an opportunity for couples and families to reinvest in their relationships and strengthen emotional bonds. The post-holiday period is often seen as a time of readjustment and getting back into a routine. It also presents an opportunity for couples and families to rejuvenate their relationships and strengthen emotional bonds. The holiday season, with its many demands and distractions, can sometimes lead to neglected relationships. Whether it is due to the busyness of holiday preparations or the stresses that can arise during family gatherings, couples and families may find themselves feeling disconnected from one another. The post-holiday period provides a valuable time to reflect and prioritize relationships. It allows couples and families to take a step back from the chaos and focus on each other, with fewer distractions to impede their efforts. This can be achieved through various means, such as setting aside dedicated time for shared activities or engaging in open and honest communication. By doing so, partners and family members can address any unresolved issues that may have arisen during the holiday season, and work towards resolving them together. The post-holiday period allows for the opportunity to create new traditions or revive old ones that may have fallen by the wayside. Engaging in shared experiences can foster a sense of belonging and strengthen emotional ties. For couples, it can be as simple as going on regular date nights or finding a new hobby to pursue together. For families, it could involve planning regular family outings or game nights. These activities not only provide opportunities for quality time spent together but also serve as a reminder of the importance of maintaining strong relationships. Strengthening emotional bonds requires more than just spending time together. It also entails actively listening to one another, showing empathy, and being supportive. The post-holiday period offers an ideal environment for such practices, as partners and family members are likely to be more receptive and willing to invest in their relationships. It is a time where individuals can reflect on their own actions and behaviors, and consider how they can contribute to the overall well-being of their relationships. The post-holiday period is not only a time for readjustment but also a valuable opportunity to reinvest in relationships and strengthen emotional bonds. By taking advantage of this period, couples and families can prioritize their relationships, address any unresolved issues, create new traditions or revive old ones, and actively engage in practices that foster connection and understanding. This rejuvenation process can lead to healthier and more fulfilling relationships for all involved.

QUALITY TIME TOGETHER

Engaging in activities that promote connection and intimacy, such as date nights or family outings, can help rekindle relationships. In the hustle and bustle of daily life, it can be easy for relationships to take a backseat. Engaging in activities that promote connection and intimacy, such as date nights or family outings, can play a crucial role in rekindling relationships. Quality time together allows individuals to reconnect on a deeper level, fostering a sense of closeness and understanding. Date nights, for instance, provide a dedicated space for couples to put aside the distractions of daily life and focus solely on each other. Whether it's going out for a romantic dinner or indulging in a shared hobby, these activities help create a sense of connection and rejuvenation. Similarly, family outings can provide a platform for strengthening bonds between parents and children. Engaging in activities together, such as going to the park or having a picnic, allows families to spend uninterrupted time with one another, fostering communication and camaraderie. Quality time also enables individuals to feel seen and heard by their loved ones, which can play a pivotal role in reducing feelings of loneliness and depression. By actively engaging in activities that promote connection and intimacy, individuals can prioritize their relationships and work towards rekindling and maintaining a strong and fulfilling bond. These activities have been found to have numerous psychological and emotional benefits, such as reducing stress and improving overall well-being. In the context of depression, quality time together can serve as an important tool in managing symptoms and improving mental health. Depression often leads to isolation and withdrawal from social interactions, making it even more essential to foster connections and promote intimacy. Engaging in activities together not only offers an opportunity for individuals to step outside their own thoughts and concerns but also provides a supportive environment where emotions can be shared and understood. By spending quality time together, partners and family members can create a safe space where individuals feel comfortable expressing themselves, ultimately aiding in the healing process.

Quality time together serves as a reminder of the positive aspects of relationships. When individuals are caught up in the daily grind, it is easy to lose sight of the reasons why they fell in love or forged strong family bonds in the first place. By engaging in activities that promote connection and intimacy, individuals are able to reconnect with these positive memories and experiences, reminding them of the love and support that their relationships offer. Quality time together is an invaluable tool in rekindling relationships, promoting emotional well-being, and managing symptoms of depression. By consciously setting aside time to engage in activities that nurture connection, couples and families can build a strong foundation of love, understanding, and support, ultimately leading to healthier and happier relationships.

PRACTICING GRATITUDE

Expressing appreciation and recognizing the positive aspects of one another can enhance relationship satisfaction.

The holiday season often brings a whirlwind of emotions and experiences, leaving individuals feeling exhausted and overwhelmed once the festivities come to an end. As routines are established and individuals return to their regular responsibilities, it becomes crucial to focus on gratitude and appreciation within relationships. Expressing gratitude allows individuals to acknowledge and value the positive aspects of their partners, friends, and family members. This practice promotes a sense of gratitude, which can lead to increased relationship satisfaction. Research has shown that expressing gratitude is linked to higher levels of well-being, both individually and within relationships. When individuals take the time to recognize and appreciate the positive qualities and actions of their loved ones, they create a harmonious atmosphere filled with love and respect. By expressing your gratitude, you not only boost your own happiness but also create a positive feedback loop in the relationship, as your partner is more likely to reciprocate the appreciation. Recognizing and expressing gratitude can help individuals navigate through challenging times, providing a sense of stability and reassurance. When faced with obstacles and stressors, expressing gratitude allows couples and family members to focus on the strengths and resources they possess, fostering resilience and unity. In addition to verbal expressions of appreciation, practices such as writing gratitude letters or keeping a gratitude journal can be utilized to reinforce positive feelings within relationships. These practices encourage individuals to reflect on the positive aspects of their loved ones, highlighting their unique qualities and contributions. Actively practicing gratitude can also counteract negative relational behaviors, such as criticism and hostility. As individuals focus on the positive aspects of their relationships, the negative aspects are minimized, leading to increased relationship satisfaction. Practicing gratitude cultivates a mindset of abundance, where individuals become more attuned to the positive experiences and moments they share with their loved ones. This mindset shift can have a profound impact on overall relationship satisfaction and happiness. Practicing gratitude and expressing appreciation are essential for maintaining healthy and satisfying relationships. By acknowledging and valuing the positive attributes of our loved ones, we create a positive and nurturing environment that fosters love, respect, and happiness. The practice of gratitude not only benefits individuals by promoting their well-being but also strengthens their relationships by fostering unity and resilience. Thus, as we transition back to our regular routines after the holidays, it is crucial to prioritize gratitude and appreciation within our relationships to enhance relationship satisfaction and overall happiness. During the holiday season, many people look forward to spending quality time with loved ones, taking a break from work or school, and indulging in festive activities. After the holidays come to an end, some individuals may experience feelings of depression, difficulty in readjusting to their daily routines, and strain in their relationships. This phenomenon, known as the post-holiday blues, can be attributed to a variety of factors. Firstly, the contrast between the joyful and lively holiday atmosphere and the mundane tasks of daily life can be quite stark, leading to a sense of emptiness or sadness. The excitement and anticipation that come with holiday traditions and celebrations can create a temporary bubble of happiness, which bursts when reality sets in. The high expectations associated with the holidays, such as finding the perfect gifts, creating the ideal atmosphere, or having meaningful interactions with others, can sometimes lead to disappointment or feelings of inadequacy once the festivities are over. This can further contribute to a sense of sadness or dissatisfaction. The return to work or school can be particularly challenging, as individuals may feel overwhelmed by the demands and responsibilities that await them. The shift from a more relaxed and carefree holiday schedule to a structured one can be difficult to navigate, causing stress and anxiety. Relationships can also be strained during this time. The constant togetherness and intense emotions experienced during the holidays can sometimes create unrealistic expectations or bring underlying issues to the surface. As the pace of life returns to normal, conflicts may arise, and the pressure to maintain the same level of closeness or intimacy experienced during the holidays can weigh heavily on individuals and their relationships. The post-holiday blues can be a challenging period for many individuals. There are steps that can be taken to mitigate these feelings and readjust to everyday life. Engaging in self-care activities, such as getting enough sleep, exercising, and practicing Mindfulness , can help to alleviate symptoms of depression and increase overall well-being. Establishing a routine and setting achievable goals can also provide a sense of structure and purpose, making the transition from the holidays to daily life easier. Open and honest communication with loved ones can help to address any conflicts or strains in relationships that may have arisen during the holidays. By acknowledging and validating these feelings, individuals can work together to find solutions and strengthen their connections. By understanding the factors that contribute to the post-holiday blues and taking proactive steps to navigate this transitional period, individuals can effectively manage their emotions, readjust to their daily routines, and foster healthier and more fulfilling relationships.

XII. PROFESSIONAL ASSISTANCE

Professional assistance can play a crucial role in helping individuals navigate the challenges of readjustment and relationships after the holiday season. For individuals struggling with depression, seeking professional help can provide the necessary support and tools to effectively manage their symptoms. Therapists, counselors, and psychologists can offer a safe and nonjudgmental space for individuals to express their emotions and explore the underlying causes of their depression. Through various therapeutic techniques, such as cognitive-behavioral therapy (CBT), individuals can learn to identify negative thought patterns and develop more positive and constructive ways of thinking. Professional assistance can help individuals develop coping strategies and self-care practices that promote overall well-being and resilience. This may include incorporating exercise, practicing Mindfulness techniques, and fostering healthy relationships. Seeking professional help can be particularly beneficial for individuals experiencing difficulties in their relationships after the holiday season. Couples counselors and relationship therapists can provide a neutral space where partners can openly communicate and work towards resolving conflicts. These professionals can offer guidance on effective communication techniques, conflict resolution skills, and strategies to rebuild trust and intimacy. By addressing underlying issues and improving communication, couples can strengthen their bond and work towards a healthier and more fulfilling relationship. Professional assistance can help individuals navigate the challenges of readjusting to their daily routines after the holiday season. Life coaches and career counselors can offer guidance and support in setting realistic goals, managing time effectively, and finding motivation and fulfillment in their work or studies. These professionals can also provide valuable insights and strategies for maintaining a work-life balance and reducing stress. Seeking professional assistance can significantly enhance an individual's ability to readjust after the holiday season and improve their relationships, mental health, and overall well-being. By collaborating with trained professionals, individuals can gain insight, acquire new skills, and develop effective coping strategies to overcome the challenges they may face. It is important to recognize that professional assistance should not be seen as a sign of weakness, but rather as a proactive step towards promoting one's mental health and fostering meaningful connections in their personal and professional lives.

THERAPY AND COUNSELING

Seeking professional assistance, such as individual or couples therapy, can assist in navigating post-holiday challenges.

The holiday season is often associated with joy and happiness. For many individuals, the period after the holidays can be an emotionally challenging time. The experience of going back to routine, coupled with the stress of readjustment, can take a toll on one's mental health and relationships. It is during this time that seeking professional assistance, such as individual or couples therapy, can be highly beneficial. Therapy and counseling provide a safe and confidential space where individuals can explore and process their emotions. Through therapy, individuals can gain insight into their feelings of depression and better understand the root causes. Therapy can equip individuals with coping strategies and tools to navigate the post-holiday challenges effectively. Couples therapy, in particular, can help address relationship difficulties that may arise during this period. The holiday season often includes increased time spent with significant others, which can either strengthen or strain a relationship. Couples therapy can provide a supportive environment where both partners can discuss their concerns and work towards resolving conflicts. Therapy allows couples to improve their communication skills and gain a deeper understanding of each other's needs and expectations. By seeking professional assistance, individuals and couples can potentially prevent the post-holiday blues from taking a toll on their well-being and relationships. Some individuals may hesitate to seek therapy due to stigmas attached to mental health concerns. They may view therapy as a sign of weakness or unnecessary intervention. It is important to recognize that therapy is a valuable tool for personal growth and healing. Therapists are trained professionals who can provide objective insights and guidance, tailored to individual needs. They offer a non-judgmental and supportive space, where individuals can freely express their emotions and concerns. Seeking therapy shows strength and a proactive approach towards one's mental health. Individual and couples therapy can make a significant difference in navigating the challenges that arise after the holidays. It can help individuals develop healthier coping mechanisms, improve their relationships, and enhance overall well-being. By addressing post-holiday challenges through therapy, individuals are more likely to achieve a smoother transition back to routine and maintain emotional stability. The post-holiday period can be challenging, but with the support of therapy, individuals can effectively overcome these challenges and cultivate a healthier mindset and relationship dynamics.

COGNITIVE-BEHAVIORAL THERAPY

CBT techniques help individuals identify and change negative thought patterns, promoting emotional well-being.

Cognitive-behavioral therapy (CBT) techniques aim to alleviate the negative impact of thought patterns on emotional well-being. Through CBT, individuals can identify their negative thoughts and replace them with more positive and constructive ones. This therapy approach recognizes the powerful influence of thoughts on emotions, behaviors, and overall mental health. By examining cognitive distortions such as all-or-nothing thinking, overgeneralization, and personalization, individuals can gain greater self-awareness and challenge their maladaptive beliefs. CBT techniques include cognitive restructuring, behavioral experiments, and thought records, all of which encourage individuals to change their negative thought patterns. For instance, cognitive restructuring helps individuals challenge and reframe their irrational beliefs and replace them with more realistic and balanced thoughts. Behavioral experiments allow individuals to test the validity of their negative beliefs, often revealing their inaccuracy. Thought records enable individuals to track their thoughts and emotions, providing a foundation for identifying recurring patterns and assessing the accuracy of their thoughts. Through these techniques, individuals learn to recognize and challenge negative thought patterns, gradually replacing them with more positive and helpful thoughts. This process promotes emotional well-being and helps individuals develop healthier coping strategies. By modifying their thoughts, individuals can experience a reduction in symptoms associated with depression and anxiety. Cognitive-behavioral therapy is widely recognized as an effective treatment for various mental health disorders, including depression and anxiety. Its emphasis on identifying and changing negative thought patterns makes it particularly valuable for individuals struggling with distorted thinking and negative self-perceptions. The therapy's collaborative and goal-oriented approach empowers individuals to take an active role in their own well-being and fosters a sense of control over their emotions and behaviors. CBT techniques can be easily integrated into one's daily life, allowing individuals to continue practicing them outside of therapy sessions. Cognitive-behavioral therapy offers individuals a powerful tool for improving their emotional well-being by challenging negative thought patterns and fostering a more positive and constructive mindset. Through its techniques, individuals can become aware of their thought patterns, identify cognitive distortions, and subsequently replace negative thoughts with more helpful and accurate ones. By promoting self-awareness and healthier thinking, cognitive-behavioral therapy equips individuals with the skills necessary to navigate life more effectively, enabling them to experience emotional well-being and improved psychological functioning.

MEDICATION OPTIONS

If necessary, working with a psychiatrist to explore medication as an adjunct to therapy may be beneficial for managing post-holiday depression. While therapy can be effective in providing individuals with coping strategies and support, there are instances where medication may be necessary to alleviate symptoms associated with post-holiday depression. Medications such as selective serotonin reuptake inhibitors (SSRIs) or serotonin-norepinephrine reuptake inhibitors (SNRIs) may be prescribed to help regulate serotonin levels in the brain and improve mood. These medications are often used in conjunction with therapy to provide a comprehensive approach to treatment. It is important to note that medication should not be seen as a solution to all problems, but rather as a tool to help individuals manage their symptoms while they work on addressing underlying issues through therapy. Working closely with a psychiatrist is essential in order to determine the most appropriate medication and dosage for each individual, as well as monitor any potential side effects. Medication can be particularly helpful for individuals who experience severe symptoms of post-holiday depression, such as persistent sadness, suicidal thoughts, or lack of motivation. In these cases, medication can provide the necessary support to stabilize mood and enable individuals to engage more effectively in therapy. It is crucial to regularly assess the effectiveness of medication in combination with therapy, as treatment plans may need to be adjusted over time. It is also important to consider potential drawbacks or limitations of medication, such as the possibility of side effects or the need for long-term use. Medication should be approached as a decision made in collaboration with a healthcare professional, taking into account an individual's specific circumstances and preferences. Exploring medication options in tandem with therapy can be beneficial for managing post-holiday depression, particularly for individuals with severe symptoms or those who have not experienced significant improvement through therapy alone. Collaborating with a psychiatrist and closely monitoring the effectiveness of medication can help individuals find the right balance between pharmacological and psychological interventions, ultimately supporting their recovery and readjustment after the holiday season.

After the holiday season comes to an end, many individuals find themselves struggling with readjustment and the mundane routine of everyday life. This transition from the excitement and festivities back to reality can be particularly challenging for individuals who suffer from depression. The abrupt change in daily activities and the absence of social engagements can worsen their symptoms and trigger feelings of sadness and loneliness. The holiday season often involves spending time with loved ones and creating cherished memories together. Saying goodbye to family and friends can be emotionally difficult, especially for individuals who rely on these relationships for support and love. The sudden absence of these connections can intensify feelings of loneliness and increase the risk of developing depressive symptoms. As individuals attempt to return to their regular routines, it is essential for them to recognize the potential impact this transition may have on their mental health and take proactive steps to maintain their emotional well-being.

One strategy for managing depression and readjusting after the holidays is to maintain a balanced routine. Establishing a consistent schedule and engaging in activities that bring joy and fulfillment can help individuals regain a sense of normalcy. This may include setting aside time for exercise, engaging in hobbies or interests, and spending quality time with loved ones. Practicing self-care is crucial during this period. Engaging in activities that promote relaxation and self-reflection, such as meditation or journaling, can help individuals process their emotions and reduce stress levels. It is also important for individuals to prioritize their mental health by seeking professional help if necessary. Therapy or counseling sessions can provide individuals with the necessary tools to cope with depressive symptoms and navigate the challenges of readjustment.

Maintaining and strengthening social connections is another essential aspect of managing depression and readjusting after the holiday season. While it may be challenging to recreate the same level of social engagement experienced during the holidays, individuals can still make an effort to connect with others. This can be as simple as reaching out to a friend for a coffee date or joining a community group or club that aligns with one's interests. By maintaining social connections, individuals can find emotional support, share their experiences and feelings, and combat feelings of loneliness. Fostering meaningful relationships can provide individuals with a sense of purpose and belonging, which is vital for their overall well-being.

Readjusting after the holiday season can be a difficult period for individuals, particularly those with depression. The sudden shift from excitement and social engagement to routine and isolation can intensify depressive symptoms and trigger feelings of sadness and loneliness. By maintaining a balanced routine, practicing self-care, and prioritizing social connections, individuals can effectively manage their depression and navigate the challenges of readjustment. It is crucial for individuals to recognize the potential impact this transition can have on their mental health and to take proactive steps to maintain their emotional well-being.

XIII. TIME FOR SELF-CARE

In today's fast-paced world, time seems to slip through our fingers, leaving little room for self-care. It is crucial to carve out moments for ourselves amidst our busy routines. Self-care is not selfish, but rather a necessary practice to replenish our physical, mental, and emotional well-being. Without taking the time to care for ourselves, we risk burnout, increased stress levels, and a decline in overall health. One area where self-care is increasingly important is in maintaining good mental health. The pressures of daily life can leave us feeling overwhelmed, stressed, and anxious. By engaging in self-care activities such as meditation, journaling, or engaging in a hobby, we can help reduce stress levels and promote mental clarity. Taking the time to disconnect from technology and reconnect with ourselves can do wonders for our mental health. Self-care is vital for nurturing healthy relationships. When we neglect our own needs, we often become depleted and are unable to give our best to our loved ones. By prioritizing self-care, we can recharge our emotional energy and show up fully present in our relationships. Whether it is enjoying quality time with loved ones, engaging in deep conversations, or simply expressing gratitude, self-care allows us to foster deeper connections and create a sense of balance in our relationships. Self-care is essential in the process of readjustment after the holiday season. The festivities and time spent with family and friends can be both joyous and exhausting. The return to routine after such a break can be challenging, and self-care can serve as a tool to ease this transition. Engaging in activities that bring us joy and relaxation, such as leisurely walks, reading, or indulging in a favorite hobby, can provide a sense of comfort and stability during this period of readjustment. Self-care is a vital aspect of our lives that should not be overlooked, especially in today's fast-paced world. Prioritizing self-care allows us to maintain good mental health, nurture healthy relationships, and ease the readjustment process after the holiday season. By taking the time to care for ourselves, we are better equipped to handle life's challenges and are better able to show up as our best selves in all areas of our lives. Self-care is not selfish; it is a necessary investment in our overall well-being.

UNDERSTANDING SELF-CARE

Practicing self-care involves engaging in activities that promote physical, emotional, and mental well-being.
Understanding self-care is crucial for individuals to maintain their overall well-being. Practicing self-care involves engaging in activities that promote physical, emotional, and mental health. Physical self-care focuses on taking care of one's body through exercise, nutrition, and rest. Engaging in regular exercise helps individuals maintain a healthy weight, strengthen their immune system, and reduce the risk of chronic disease. Eating a balanced diet that includes fruits, vegetables, whole grains, and lean proteins provides the necessary nutrients to sustain a healthy body. Adequate rest is equally important, as it allows the body to rejuvenate and repair itself. Emotional self-care involves acknowledging and addressing one's emotions in a healthy and constructive manner. This can be achieved through activities such as journaling, meditation, or seeking therapy. Journaling allows individuals to reflect on their thoughts and feelings, providing an outlet for self-expression. Meditation, on the other hand, helps individuals focus on the present moment, calming their minds and reducing stress. Seeking therapy provides individuals with a safe space to navigate and understand their emotions, enabling them to develop coping mechanisms and build resilience. Mental self-care focuses on maintaining and improving cognitive functions. Engaging in activities that challenge the mind, such as reading, puzzles, or learning new skills, promotes mental wellness. Reading stimulates the brain, enhances vocabulary, and cultivates criti-

cal thinking skills. Puzzles, such as crosswords or sudoku, exercise the brain and improve memory and problem-solving abilities. Learning new skills, whether it be playing an instrument or studying a new language, not only keeps the mind active but also provides a sense of accomplishment and personal growth. Understanding self-care is essential for individuals to lead a balanced and fulfilling life. Engaging in activities that promote physical, emotional, and mental well-being is crucial for maintaining overall health. By prioritizing self-care, individuals can take proactive steps towards improving their quality of life and establishing healthy habits that will benefit them in the long run.

IDENTIFYING SELF-CARE STRATEGIES

Individuals can explore various activities, such as exercise, meditation, or hobbies, to identify self-care methods that suit their needs. Identifying self-care strategies is crucial for individuals to navigate their emotional well-being and maintain a healthy routine, especially after the holiday season. One effective self-care method that individuals can explore is exercise. Engaging in physical activities not only improves one's physical health but also has a positive impact on mental well-being. Exercise helps release endorphins, which are known as "feel-good" hormones, leading to elevated mood and reducing stress levels. By incorporating exercise into their daily routines, individuals can cultivate a sense of balance and rejuvenation, enabling them to effectively tackle the challenges of readjusting after the holidays. In addition to exercise, individuals can turn to meditation as a self-care strategy. Meditation is a practice that focuses on calming the mind and observing one's thoughts without judgment. Through meditation, individuals can gain a deeper understanding of themselves, their emotions, and their present moment experiences. By setting aside time each day for meditation, individuals can enhance their self-awareness, develop a greater sense of clarity, and reduce anxiety. The ability to be present and mindful can be particularly valuable during the post-holiday period when individuals may be experiencing a range of emotions and struggling to find their equilibrium.

Exploring hobbies can be an effective way for individuals to identify self-care methods that suit their needs. Engaging in activities that bring joy and fulfillment can provide a therapeutic outlet and help individuals reconnect with their passions. Whether it is painting, playing a musical instrument, or gardening, hobbies can serve as a form of self-expression and be a source of solace during moments of stress or transition. Discovering and dedicating time to hobbies can invigorate individuals' lives by promoting creativity, unleashing hidden talents, and creating a renewed sense of purpose and achievement.

Identifying suitable self-care strategies is essential to preserve emotional well-being and readjust after the holiday season. Exercise, meditation, and engaging in hobbies are all potential avenues for individuals to explore and find methods that best suit their needs. By incorporating exercise into their routine, individuals can cultivate a sense of balance and rejuvenation. Meditation can provide individuals with a deeper understanding of themselves and their emotions, helping them navigate the challenges of transitioning out of the holiday season. Exploring hobbies can provide individuals with a therapeutic outlet and help them reconnect with their passions. By taking care of oneself through these self-care strategies, individuals can effectively manage their emotional well-being and successfully navigate the post-holiday period.

PRIORITIZING SELF-CARE

Making self-care a priority, even during the post-holiday rush, fosters resilience and supports overall mental health.

During the post-holiday rush, it is imperative to prioritize self-care in order to foster resilience and support overall mental health. The hustle and bustle that follows the holiday season can often leave individuals feeling overwhelmed and drained, making it all the more important to dedicate time and energy to taking care of oneself. Prioritizing self-care can look different for each individual, as it is a deeply personal practice that should cater to one's unique needs and preferences. It may involve engaging in activities that bring joy and fulfillment, such as practicing yoga, reading a book, or spending quality time with loved ones. Engaging in these activities can provide individuals with a sense of calm and relaxation, allowing them to recharge their batteries and regain a sense of balance. Prioritizing self-care can involve setting boundaries and learning to say no to commitments or responsibilities that may be causing undue stress or anxiety. By doing so, individuals can create space in their lives for rest and rejuvenation, enabling them to better cope with the demands of daily life. Self-care can involve seeking professional help when needed, such as consulting a therapist or counselor. These trained professionals can provide invaluable support and guidance, offering tools and strategies to help individuals navigate through challenges and improve their mental well-being. By actively prioritizing self-care, individuals are investing in their own mental health and building resilience to better cope with the inevitable ups and downs of life. Regular self-care practices not only foster emotional well-being but also contribute to a healthier overall lifestyle. Making self-care a priority during the post-holiday rush is crucial in maintaining a sense of balance and reducing the risk of experiencing depression or burnout. Through self-care, individuals can mitigate the negative effects of stress and prevent it from accumulating and taking a toll on their mental health. Prioritizing self-care in the midst of the post-holiday rush is essential for fostering resilience and supporting overall mental health. By dedicating time and energy to engage in activities that bring joy and fulfillment, setting boundaries, seeking professional help when needed, individuals can better cope with the demands of life and maintain a sense of balance. Practicing self-care not only benefits one's mental well-being but also contributes to a healthier and more fulfilling life. The post-holiday season can often bring about a wave of emotions for individuals as they grapple with readjusting to their regular routines. For some, this transition can be particularly challenging, as they may find themselves experiencing feelings of depression and struggling to maintain their relationships. The holiday season is often filled with joy, excitement, and time spent with loved ones. Once the festivities come to an end, individuals are thrust back into their everyday lives, which can feel mundane and lackluster in comparison. This abrupt change can be a significant trigger for depression, as individuals may find it difficult to find purpose and meaning in their daily activities. The pressure to return to work or school after a long break can also contribute to these depressive feelings, as individuals may feel overwhelmed and stressed by the demands of their responsibilities. In addition to the individual's struggle with depression, readjustment after the holidays can also put a strain on relationships. During the holiday season, individuals often spend more time with their loved ones, enjoying quality time together and creating lasting memories. Once the holidays are over, these connections may diminish as individuals return to their own pursuits and responsibilities. This can create a sense of distance and disconnect within relationships, which can be challenging to navigate. Couples may find themselves struggling to find time for each other amidst their busy schedules, causing frustration and feelings of neglect to arise. Friends may also experience a similar strain, as they try to balance their individual commitments while still maintaining their friendships. The readjustment period after the holidays requires individuals to find a way to navigate these challenges and find a sense of balance and contentment in their everyday lives. To combat feelings of depression, individuals can try to set small goals or create a sense of purpose in their everyday activities. This can involve finding joy in the simple moments, such as engaging in a hobby or spending time with loved ones. Seeking support from a therapist or counselor can also be helpful in managing and overcoming depressive feelings. When it comes to relationships, communication and prioritization are key. Couples can try to schedule regular date nights or find activities they enjoy doing together to help maintain their connection. Friends can also make an effort to reach out and plan gatherings or outings, ensuring that they continue to nurture their friendships. It's essential for individuals to understand that readjustment after the holidays is a normal process that often requires time and effort. By acknowledging and addressing these challenges, individuals can navigate this transitional period and find a sense of stability and fulfillment in their day-to-day lives.

XIV. REEVALUATING EXPECTATIONS

As the holiday season comes to an end, it becomes crucial to reevaluate our expectations. The festivities filled with joy, love, and togetherness often create a distorted image of what our everyday lives should be like. We find ourselves comparing our own realities to the idealized versions we see on social media or in movies. It is essential to understand that real life is not a constant celebration but a series of ups and downs. This discrepancy between our expectations and reality can often lead to feelings of disappointment and discontentment, making it crucial to readjust our outlook. Society has conditioned us to believe that happiness is a constant state of being. We are bombarded with images of perfect relationships, successful careers, and a glamorous lifestyle. This constant exposure can create unrealistic expectations for ourselves and others. We often forget that life is a complex journey filled with both triumphs and tribulations. By reevaluating our expectations, we can shed the unnecessary pressure we place on ourselves to conform to an idealized version of happiness.

Reevaluating our expectations also involves understanding the importance of self-compassion. It is easy to fall into the trap of self-criticism when our lives do not match our expectations. It is important to remember that we are all human beings with flaws, limitations, and imperfections. Instead of berating ourselves for not living up to our own expectations, we should practice self-love and acceptance. By being kind to ourselves, we can foster a more positive and nurturing environment for personal growth and happiness. Reevaluating our expectations allows for a more realistic understanding of relationships. The holiday season often portrays idealized versions of love and togetherness. Real relationships are not always picture-perfect. They require effort, compromise, and occasional disagreements. By acknowledging the imperfect nature of relationships, we can cultivate a more authentic and fulfilling connection with our loved ones. Reevaluating our expectations also helps us recognize the importance of open communication and setting healthy boundaries, fostering long-lasting and meaningful relationships. As the holiday season fades away, it is crucial to reevaluate our expectations. The festivities often paint an unrealistic image of what our lives should look like, causing feelings of disappointment and discontentment when reality does not match these ideals. By reassessing our outlook, embracing self-compassion, and understanding the true nature of relationships, we can cultivate a more realistic and fulfilling approach to life. Let us strive to find happiness in the everyday moments and embrace the journey that life presents us with, rather than constantly chasing an unattainable ideal.

CHALLENGING EXPECTATIONS

Unmet holiday expectations can contribute to feelings of disappointment and post-holiday depression.

Unmet holiday expectations can contribute to feelings of disappointment and post-holiday depression. During the holiday season, there is often an underlying excitement and anticipation for joyous celebrations, quality time with loved ones, and a break from the usual routine. When these expectations are not met, it can lead to a sense of disillusionment and sadness. This can occur when individuals have unrealistic expectations of how the holidays should unfold or when they have specific hopes for certain experiences or outcomes that do not materialize. For example, someone may have expected to have a picture-perfect holiday gathering with their family, filled with laughter and warmth, only to find themselves in an uncomfortable or tense situation. Alternatively, an individual may have hoped for a significant other to propose during the holidays, hoping to solidify their relationship, but instead, they were met with disappointment and a sense of rejection. In these instances, the contrast between what was envisioned and what actually occurred can bring about a great deal of sadness and frustration, contributing to post-holiday depression. Societal expectations and the pressures to meet societal norms during the holiday season can add another layer of stress to individuals. There is often an emphasis on extravagant gift-giving, elaborate decorations, and picturesque holiday experiences. When individuals feel unable to meet these societal expectations, they may feel a sense of failure and self-judgment, leading to negative emotions and a diminished sense of self-worth. The transition from the high of the holiday season back to the regular routine of daily life can exacerbate these feelings of disappointment and sadness. The abrupt change from a time filled with festivities, warmth, and connection to the mundanity of everyday life can be jarring and calls attention to the contrast between what was experienced during the holidays and what is expected in the normal day-to-day routine. This shift can leave individuals feeling unfulfilled and longing for the joy and excitement that was present during the holiday season. Unmet holiday expectations can contribute significantly to post-holiday depression. The disparity between the anticipated and the actual experiences during the holidays, the pressure to meet societal expectations, and the subsequent return to routine life all play a role in generating these feelings of disappointment. It is essential for individuals to be mindful of their expectations during the holiday season and to prioritize self-care and self-compassion, as they navigate the transition back to routine and work to manage any post-holiday depression that may arise.

REALISTIC GOAL-SETTING

Reevaluating and setting realistic expectations promotes a more balanced approach to future holiday seasons.

As the holiday season comes to an end, many individuals find themselves feeling overwhelmed and dissatisfied with their experiences. This dissatisfaction often stems from unrealistic expectations set for the holiday season, such as wanting everything to be perfect or trying to accommodate everyone's needs and desires. It is important to recognize that the holiday season is just like any other time of the year, and it is unrealistic to expect everything to go smoothly and perfectly. By reevaluating these expectations and setting more realistic goals for future holiday seasons, individuals can avoid the trap of feeling disappointed and overwhelmed. Realistic goal-setting allows for a more balanced approach to the holidays, where individuals can focus on what truly matters and let go of unnecessary stress and pressure. For example, instead of trying to please everyone by hosting extravagant parties and events, individuals might choose to prioritize spending quality time with loved ones and focusing on meaningful connections. By setting these more attainable goals, individuals can experience a greater sense of satisfaction and fulfillment during the holiday season.

Realistic goal-setting also plays an essential role in maintaining mental and emotional well-being during and after the holidays. Unrealistic expectations often lead to increased stress levels, as individuals may feel overwhelmed by the pressure to meet societal standards or fulfill certain traditions. This heightened stress can negatively impact mental health, leading to symptoms of anxiety and depression. By reevaluating expectations and setting more realistic goals, individuals can reduce stress and promote a healthier mindset. For instance, instead of striving for perfection in every aspect of the holiday season, individuals might focus on self-care and prioritizing their mental well-being. This approach allows individuals to set boundaries, manage their time and energy effectively, and allocate resources in a way that supports their overall emotional health.

Reevaluating and setting realistic expectations is crucial in promoting a more balanced approach to future holiday seasons. By recognizing that perfection is unattainable and that it is okay to prioritize self-care and meaningful connections over extravagant events and traditions, individuals can avoid feeling overwhelmed and dissatisfied. Realistic goal-setting not only helps in managing stress and maintaining mental well-being but also allows individuals to experience a greater sense of satisfaction and fulfillment during the holiday season. As we move forward from the holidays and back into our regular routines, it is essential to reflect on our experiences and reassess our expectations to ensure a more realistic and positive approach to future holiday seasons.

FOCUSING ON GRATITUDE

Cultivating a sense of gratitude for what was enjoyed during the holidays instead of dwelling on unmet expectations helps reframe the post-holiday mindset.

The holiday season often comes with immense pressure to create the perfect experience filled with laughter, joy, and cherished memories. The reality is that not every expectation is met, and this can leave individuals feeling empty and disappointed once the holidays are over. Rather than focusing on what went wrong or what was not accomplished, shifting the mindset towards gratitude can be a powerful tool in finding satisfaction and contentment during the post-holiday period.

By cultivating a sense of gratitude, individuals begin to recognize and appreciate the positive aspects of their holiday experience. This may include moments of connection and love shared with family and friends, the pleasure of indulging in delicious food, the beauty of holiday decorations, or the opportunity to take a break from work and enjoy leisure time. In doing so, individuals are able to acknowledge and celebrate the joyful moments they did experience, rather than dwelling on what they did not. By reframing the post-holiday mindset through gratitude, individuals can find a newfound sense of satisfaction and fulfillment, even if the holidays did not meet their initial expectations. Focusing on gratitude can also help individuals develop a more positive outlook on life in general. Research has shown that practicing gratitude can lead to increased happiness, higher levels of life satisfaction, and improved mental well-being. By actively acknowledging and appreciating the positive aspects of one's life, individuals are able to shift their attention away from negative emotions and thoughts. This change in perspective allows them to cultivate a sense of hope and optimism, leading to a more fulfilled and content existence.

Focusing on gratitude can foster stronger relationships and connections with others. By expressing gratitude towards loved ones for their presence and contributions during the holiday season, individuals can deepen the bonds of love and appreciation. This can create a positive cycle of gratitude and reciprocity, enhancing relationships and promoting a sense of belonging and connectedness. Instead of dwelling on unmet expectations, it is more beneficial to focus on cultivating a sense of gratitude for what was enjoyed during the holidays. Shifting the mindset towards gratitude allows individuals to appreciate the positive aspects of their holiday experience and find fulfillment in the moments of joy shared with loved ones. Practicing gratitude can lead to a more positive outlook on life and foster stronger relationships. By reframing the post-holiday mindset through gratitude, individuals can navigate the transition back to routine with a sense of contentment and optimism.

The period immediately following the holiday season can be a challenging time for many individuals. After the excitement and camaraderie of the holidays, the return to routine can often trigger feelings of depression and a sense of loss. One of the reasons for this is the contrast between the joyful, festive atmosphere of the holidays and the mundane, everyday tasks that typify our daily lives. The holidays bring with them a sense of togetherness, as families and friends gather to celebrate and enjoy each other's company. Once the decorations are taken down and the festivities have ended, people often find themselves feeling isolated and disconnected. This can be particularly difficult for those who rely on the holiday season as a time of respite from challenging circumstances or problems in their relationships. For example, individuals who are in strained or unhealthy relationships may find temporary relief during the holidays as they are often surrounded by loved ones and distractions from their issues. Once the holiday season ends, they are forced to confront their problems once again, which can lead to feelings of hopelessness and sadness. Readjusting to the demands and responsibilities of work or school after a period of relaxation can also be mentally and emotionally taxing. The sudden shift from a carefree and leisurely lifestyle to a structured and demanding routine can cause feelings of stress and overwhelm. This is especially true for college students who have just returned from their winter break, as they are often faced with the pressure of academic deadlines and the prospect of starting a new semester. The combination of these factors can contribute to a sense of unease and discontentment, making the transition back to routine a difficult one. Thankfully, there are strategies that can help individuals navigate this challenging period. Engaging in self-care practices such as exercise, maintaining a healthy diet, and getting enough sleep can help to alleviate feelings of depression and anxiety. Seeking support from friends, family, or professional counselors can also be beneficial, as talking through one's emotions and concerns can provide perspective and validation. It is important to remember that the post-holiday readjustment period is temporary, and with time, things will begin to feel more normal again. By taking proactive steps to care for oneself and by seeking support when needed, individuals can successfully navigate the challenges that accompany the return to routine after the holidays, ultimately finding stability and contentment in their everyday lives.

XV. RESTORING PHYSICAL HEALTH

Physical health plays a crucial role in our overall well-being, and after the holiday season, it is essential to prioritize its restoration. During this festive time, we may have indulged in decadent meals, skipped exercise routines, and neglected our bodies' need for rest. Now, as we transition back to our daily routines, it is vital to incorporate healthy habits that promote physical well-being. One avenue to restore physical health is through nutrition. Consuming a balanced diet rich in whole grains, fruits, vegetables, and lean protein can help replenish our bodies with essential vitamins and minerals. It is crucial to limit our intake of processed foods, sugars, and unhealthy fats that can have detrimental effects on our bodies over time. Adequate hydration is also vital, as it aids in digestion, regulates body temperature, and supports healthy organ function. It is recommended to drink an adequate amount of water daily. Regular exercise is paramount in restoring physical health. Engaging in activities such as aerobic exercises, strength training, and flexibility exercises can help improve cardiovascular health, build muscle strength, and increase flexibility. Exercise also contributes to the release of endorphins, which can elevate our mood, reduce stress, and improve overall mental well-being. Incorporating exercise into a daily routine can be achieved by setting realistic goals, finding activities that bring joy, and gradually increasing intensity and duration. Another aspect of restoring physical health is ensuring adequate sleep. The holiday season often disrupts our sleep patterns, resulting in restlessness and fatigue. Establishing a consistent sleep schedule, avoiding caffeine and electronic devices before bedtime, and creating a tranquil sleep environment can aid in restoring quality sleep. Sleep not only allows our bodies to recover and rejuvenate but also enhances cognitive function, mood, and immune system function. Practicing self-care is essential for restoring physical health. Engaging in activities such as meditation, deep breathing exercises, and spending time in nature can promote relaxation, reduce stress levels, and improve overall well-being. Taking the time to engage in hobbies or activities that bring pleasure can contribute to our physical health by reducing stress and fostering a sense of fulfillment. Restoring physical health after the holidays requires a multifaceted approach that encompasses nutrition, exercise, sleep, and self-care. By prioritizing these aspects, we can gradually reintegrate healthy habits into our daily routines, improve our physical well-being, and set a solid foundation for overall vitality and success.

BALANCING NUTRITION

After indulging in festive treats, focusing on a balanced diet restores physical health and provides energy for readjustment. After the holiday season, it is common for individuals to have indulged in various festive treats that are often high in calories and low in nutritional value. In order to restore physical health and provide energy for readjustment, it is crucial to focus on a balanced diet. A balanced diet consists of a variety of foods that provide essential nutrients such as vitamins, minerals, proteins, carbohydrates, and healthy fats. By including a wide range of nutrient-dense foods in one's diet, individuals can ensure that their bodies receive the necessary fuel to function optimally. This not only helps in maintaining a healthy weight but also improves overall well-being. Consuming a balanced diet has been linked to a reduced risk of chronic diseases such as heart disease, diabetes, and certain types of cancers. A balanced diet plays a vital role in boosting the immune system, which can be especially beneficial after the holiday period when the body may be in need of a nutritional boost. By incorporating fruits, vegetables, whole grains, lean proteins, and healthy fats into one's diet, individuals can enhance their body's ability to fight off infections and promote healing. A balanced diet can have a positive impact on mental health. Research suggests that certain nutrients, such as omega-3 fatty acids found in fatty fish, have been associated with a reduced risk of depression and cognitive decline. Consuming a variety of fruits and vegetables, which are rich in antioxidants, can help combat oxidative stress and inflammation in the body, both of which have been implicated in mental health disorders. By focusing on a balanced diet, individuals can not only replenish their physical health but also support their mental well-being during the readjustment period. After indulging in festive treats, it is essential to prioritize a balanced diet in order to restore physical health and provide energy for readjustment. A balanced diet not only ensures the intake of essential nutrients but also reduces the risk of chronic diseases, boosts the immune system, and supports mental well-being. By incorporating a variety of nutrient-dense foods into one's diet, individuals can promote overall health and successfully transition back to their routines after the holiday season.

REGULAR EXERCISE

Engaging in physical activity improves mood, reduces stress, and boosts energy levels as individuals transition back to their regular routines. The holiday season often brings about a sense of joy and excitement, with individuals indulging in delicious meals and spending quality time with loved ones. As the festivities wind down and people return to their daily routines, sometimes a sense of gloom and sadness can set in. Engaging in regular exercise can be a powerful tool in combating post-holiday blues and readjusting to a normal routine. The benefits of exercise on mental health cannot be overstated. Physical activity stimulates the production of brain chemicals such as endorphins, which are known to enhance mood and promote a sense of well-being. Exercise has been shown to reduce stress levels by decreasing the production of stress hormones, such as cortisol, and promoting relaxation. As individuals transition back to their regular routines, the demands of daily life can sometimes feel overwhelming. Engaging in regular exercise can help alleviate stress by providing an outlet for pent-up emotions and anxieties. Exercise has been found to boost energy levels, providing individuals with the physical and mental stamina needed to tackle everyday tasks. The physical exertion of exercise increases blood flow and oxygen to the brain, which can enhance cognitive function and focus. This increase in energy can be especially beneficial to those who may be experiencing fatigue or lethargy as they readjust to their regular routines after the holiday season. Regular exercise can also have long-term benefits for mental health. Studies have shown that individuals who engage in regular physical activity have a reduced risk of developing depression and anxiety disorders. Exercise can serve as a form of preventive medicine, acting as a protective factor against mental health issues. By incorporating exercise into their daily routines, individuals can build resilience and improve their overall well-being. Regular exercise is a valuable tool for individuals as they transition back to their regular routines after the holiday season. By improving mood, reducing stress, and boosting energy levels, exercise can help combat post-holiday blues and provide individuals with the physical and mental stamina needed to readjust to their daily lives. As a form of preventive medicine, exercise can also have long-term benefits for mental health. By prioritizing physical activity, individuals can enhance their overall well-being and maintain a positive mindset as they navigate the challenges of everyday life.

SUFFICIENT SLEEP

Prioritizing adequate sleep allows for better cognitive functioning and emotional regulation during the post-holiday period. Sufficient sleep is a critical component when it comes to improving cognitive functioning and emotional regulation during the post-holiday period. After the hustle and bustle of the holidays and the disruption of regular routines, it is important to prioritize getting enough sleep to ensure optimal well-being. Adequate sleep enables the brain to restore and repair itself, allowing for better cognitive performance. Research has consistently shown that lack of sleep negatively impacts attention, concentration, memory, and decision-making abilities. By allowing ourselves enough time to sleep, we are giving our brains the opportunity to recharge and function at their best. This is particularly important during the post-holiday period when we may already be feeling mentally drained from the demands and stressors of the previous weeks. Sufficient sleep plays a vital role in emotional regulation. When we don't get enough sleep, our emotional resilience can be compromised, making it more difficult to cope with the ups and downs of daily life. Lack of sleep has been linked to increased levels of irritability, mood swings, and even symptoms of depression and anxiety. By prioritizing adequate sleep, we are better equipped to handle the challenges that may arise as we readjust to our regular routines after the holidays. Establishing a consistent sleep schedule and practicing good sleep hygiene can support this process. Consistency is key when it comes to sleep, and maintaining a regular bedtime and wake-up time can help regulate our internal body clocks. Creating a sleep-friendly environment by keeping our sleeping area dark, quiet, and comfortable can promote more restful sleep. Practicing relaxation techniques before bed, such as deep breathing or meditation, can help calm the mind and promote a more peaceful transition into sleep. Sufficient sleep is paramount for optimal cognitive functioning and emotional regulation during the post-holiday period. Prioritizing and consciously making an effort to get enough sleep not only allows our brains to perform at their best but also helps us navigate the emotional challenges that may arise as we return to our regular routines. By recognizing the importance of sleep and implementing strategies to ensure adequate rest, we can set ourselves up for success in maintaining our mental and emotional well-being after the holiday season.

The holiday season is often seen as a time of joy and celebration, but for many individuals, it can also be a period of increased stress and anxiety. Coming off the excitement and busyness of the holidays, many people may find themselves feeling a sense of letdown and emptiness as they return to their normal routines. This transition can be particularly challenging for individuals who struggle with depression, as the holiday season often provides a temporary distraction from their symptoms. Returning to a regular routine can bring these symptoms back to the forefront, leaving individuals feeling overwhelmed and hopeless. In addition to the impact on mental health, the post-holiday period can also strain relationships. During the holiday season, individuals may spend more time with family and friends, creating a sense of connection and belonging. As the holidays come to an end, people often return to their everyday lives, becoming caught up in work, school, and other responsibilities. This shift in focus can leave some feeling isolated and disconnected from their loved ones, contributing to feelings of loneliness and sadness. The process of readjustment after the holidays can bring about a sense of dissatisfaction and dissatisfaction with the current state of one's life. The contrast between the joy and excitement of the holiday season and the mundane tasks of everyday life can highlight the areas in which individuals feel unfulfilled or dissatisfied. This feeling of discontentment can be especially strong for individuals who have unresolved issues or unmet goals, as the pressure to start the new year on a positive note can intensify these feelings. The post-holiday period can be a difficult and challenging time for many individuals. The return to routine can trigger symptoms of depression, strain relationships, and increase feelings of dissatisfaction. It is important for individuals to recognize these challenges and take steps to mitigate their impact. This may include seeking professional help for depression symptoms, prioritizing self-care and maintaining a consistent routine, or engaging in open and honest communication with loved ones. By acknowledging and addressing the challenges of the post-holiday period, individuals can work towards a smoother transition, better mental health, and stronger relationships.

XVI. MAINTAINING MINDFULNESS

Maintaining Mindfulness is crucial for individuals who are dealing with depression, navigating relationships, and readjusting after the holidays. Mindfulness , defined as the intentional act of being fully present in the moment without judgment, can help alleviate symptoms of depression and promote emotional well-being. By remaining aware of our thoughts, feelings, and bodily sensations, we can better identify and manage negative emotions or triggers that may arise during this time. Mindfulness also enables individuals to develop a deeper understanding and acceptance of their current circumstances, which is essential when readjusting after the holidays. Through Mindfulness , individuals can cultivate a non-reactive and non-judgmental attitude towards their thoughts and emotions, allowing them to navigate challenging situations in relationships with clarity and empathy. In order to maintain Mindfulness , several strategies can be implemented into daily routines. First, individuals can engage in Mindfulness meditation, a practice that involves sitting quietly and focusing one's attention on the breath, bodily sensations, or present moment experiences. This practice cultivates an increased awareness of one's thoughts and emotions, allowing individuals to observe them without judgment. Incorporating Mindfulness into everyday activities can also be beneficial. For example, when eating, individuals can pay attention to the taste, smell, and texture of their food, savoring each bite and acknowledging the nourishment it provides. By engaging in these daily activities with intention and attention, individuals are able to shift their focus away from rumination and worry, reducing symptoms of depression and promoting a sense of well-being. Another approach to maintaining Mindfulness is through the practice of gratitude. By consciously focusing on what one is grateful for, individuals can shift their attention away from negative thoughts and cultivate positive emotions. This practice can be incorporated into daily life by keeping a gratitude journal or expressing gratitude towards oneself and others. In relationships, gratitude plays a vital role as it fosters mutual appreciation, deepens connections, and promotes over-all relationship satisfaction. By expressing gratitude to our loved ones, we strengthen the emotional bond and create an atmosphere conducive to open and effective communication. This, in turn, aids in readjustment after the holidays, as individuals can openly express their emotions and needs, fostering understanding and support within their relationships.

Maintaining Mindfulness is essential for individuals dealing with depression, navigating relationships, and readjusting after the holidays. Incorporating Mindfulness into daily routines through practices such as meditation and gratitude can alleviate symptoms of depression, enhance emotional well-being, and promote healthy relationships. By staying present in the moment, individuals can cultivate a non-reactive and non-judgmental attitude towards their thoughts and emotions, allowing them to navigate challenging situations with clarity and empathy. The practice of Mindfulness is a valuable tool that can significantly contribute to one's overall mental health and well-being.

BENEFITS OF MINDFULNESS

Practicing Mindfulness enhances self-awareness, reduces stress, and cultivates a sense of presence in daily activities. Practicing Mindfulness is known to have numerous benefits that can greatly enhance an individual's overall well-being. One of the key advantages of Mindfulness is the way it enhances self-awareness. By paying attention to our thoughts, emotions, and bodily sensations without judgment, we gain a deeper understanding of ourselves. This self-awareness allows us to identify negative thinking patterns or destructive behaviors, enabling us to make positive changes and cultivate a healthier mindset. Mindfulness reduces stress levels by helping individuals focus on the present moment instead of dwelling on past regrets or anxieties about the future. By practicing Mindfulness meditation, individuals learn to observe their thoughts and feelings as temporary events rather than becoming entangled in them. This detachment from negative thoughts not only reduces stress but also provides individuals with a greater sense of control over their emotions. Mindfulness cultivates a sense of presence in daily activities, allowing individuals to fully engage with their surroundings and experiences. Instead of feeling detached or distracted, individuals who practice Mindfulness are fully present in the here and now, whether it be while eating a meal, walking in nature, or engaging in conversation. This increased presence heightens our ability to appreciate the simple joys of life and fosters deeper connections with others.

By being actively present, we become better listeners, more empathetic individuals, and more attuned to the needs of those around us. The deliberate and non-judgmental focus that Mindfulness encourages also translates into improved concentration and performance in tasks. Through the practice of Mindfulness , individuals can train their minds to stay present and focused, which can enhance productivity and efficiency. The practice of Mindfulness offers a wide range of benefits, including enhanced self-awareness, reduced stress levels, and a heightened sense of presence in daily activities. By incorporating Mindfulness into our lives, we can cultivate a greater understanding of ourselves, reduce stress, and approach each moment with a greater sense of presence and appreciation. Whether it be through Mindfulness meditation or cultivating Mindfulness in daily activities, the advantages gained from practicing Mindfulness are numerous and can significantly improve overall well-being and life satisfaction.

MINDFUL MOMENTS

Incorporating brief Mindfulness exercises, such as deep breathing or focused attention, throughout the day promotes mental clarity and emotional balance. In today's fast-paced society, finding moments of peace and tranquility can be challenging. With the ongoing hustle and bustle, it becomes increasingly important to carve out time for self-care and mental rejuvenation. One effective way to achieve this is through the incorporation of brief Mindfulness exercises throughout the day. These exercises, such as deep breathing or focused attention, promote mental clarity and emotional balance, allowing individuals to better navigate the challenges that come their way. By engaging in these mindful moments, individuals can pause and set aside the worries and stressors that may be plaguing their minds. Taking a deep breath in and exhaling slowly, one can promote a sense of calm and focus. This simple act allows individuals to shift their attention from racing thoughts and negative emotions to the present moment. By anchoring oneself in the here and now, individuals can better prioritize their mental well-being. In addition to deep breathing, incorporating focused attention exercises provides an opportunity to sharpen mental clarity and improve cognitive function. Focusing on a specific task or object can help individuals to develop concentration skills and reduce distractions. This often leads to enhanced productivity and efficiency in daily tasks. In fact, research has shown that individuals who engage in Mindfulness practices experience improved attention and working memory. These exercises also have the potential to promote emotional balance. By pausing throughout the day to focus on the breath or engage in mindful activities, individuals can gain a deeper understanding of their emotions and develop a healthier relationship with them. This self-awareness allows individuals to recognize and acknowledge their emotions without becoming overwhelmed by them. By taking the time to observe and accept their emotions, individuals can cultivate greater resilience and adaptability in the face of adversity. Mindfulness exercises can improve individuals' overall well-being and relationships. By promoting mental clarity, emotional balance, and self-awareness, individuals are better equipped to handle the challenges that arise in their personal and professional lives. Mindful moments provide an opportunity for individuals to nurture their mental and emotional health, resulting in healthier relationships with loved ones and increased satisfaction in their daily interactions. As individuals incorporate brief Mindfulness exercises into their routines, they can create a positive cycle of self-care and self-improvement. This practice of Mindfulness ultimately leads to a higher quality of life, increased productivity, and improved overall well-being. It is essential for individuals to prioritize these brief moments of Mindfulness throughout their day, as they have the power to transform their mindset and enhance their overall quality of life.

MINDFULNESS ROUTINES

Establishing regular Mindfulness practices, such as meditation or yoga, aids in maintaining a centered mindset during the post-holiday period. Establishing regular Mindfulness practices, such as meditation or yoga, aids in maintaining a centered mindset during the post-holiday period. The holiday season is often filled with joy, celebration, and a break from one's usual routine. As the festivities come to an end, individuals may find themselves struggling to readjust to their regular lives, leading to feelings of sadness or even depression. Engaging in Mindfulness routines can serve as a helpful tool in combating these post-holiday blues. Meditation, for instance, allows individuals to focus on the present moment and quiet their minds, which can help alleviate stress and promote a sense of calmness. By taking the time to sit in silence and simply observe their thoughts and feelings without judgment, individuals can gain a better understanding of their emotions and promote a more positive outlook. Similarly, incorporating yoga into one's routine can also contribute to a more centered mindset. Yoga combines physical movement and breathing exercises that can help reduce anxiety, increase self-awareness, and improve overall mental well-being. Participating in a yoga class or joining a meditation group can provide individuals with a sense of community and support during this transitional period. These Mindfulness practices can serve as a source of stability and routine in the post-holiday period, helping individuals find solace and peace amidst the chaos of readjustment. The regularity of these practices also allows individuals to incorporate them into their daily lives, making them more accessible and easy to maintain. By making Mindfulness routines a part of one's regular schedule, individuals can benefit from the positive effects of these practices long after the holiday season has concluded. These practices can also enhance relationships and promote emotional well-being. By cultivating self-awareness and a sense of inner peace, individuals are better equipped to handle stressors in their relationships and respond to conflicts with empathy and understanding. This can lead to healthier and more fulfilling connections with loved ones, both during the post-holiday period and beyond. Establishing regular Mindfulness practices, such as meditation or yoga, can contribute to maintaining a centered mindset during the post-holiday period. By taking the time to engage in these practices, individuals can alleviate stress, promote self-awareness, and improve overall mental well-being. By incorporating Mindfulness into their daily routines, individuals can enhance their relationships and cultivate a sense of inner peace that lasts beyond the holiday season. These practices serve as a valuable tool in navigating the readjustment process and finding stability amidst the challenges of post-holiday life. After the excitement and festivities of the holiday season, many individuals find themselves struggling with a sense of sadness and readjustment. This phenomenon, known as Post-Holiday Blues, can be attributed to a variety of factors such as the end of vacations, returning to work or school, and the anticipation of a new year. Although it is normal to experience some level of melancholy once the holiday season is over, for some individuals, these feelings may develop into a more serious condition, such as depression. Depression is a mental health disorder characterized by persistent sadness, loss of interest in activities, changes in appetite or sleep patterns, and feelings of worthlessness or guilt. It can be exacerbated by the stress and pressure to resume a daily routine, particularly in the context of relationships. One of the key challenges individuals face when readjusting to routine after the holidays is maintaining healthy relationships. During the holiday season, people often have more time and energy to invest in their relationships, whether it be spending quality time with loved ones or reconnecting with friends and family members. There is often a sense of togetherness and celebration that can be uplifting and fulfilling. Once the holiday season ends, individuals may struggle to maintain the same level of connection and support in their relationships. This can lead to feelings of isolation and loneliness, which are common triggers for depression.

Another factor that contributes to the development of depression after the holidays is the loss of excitement and anticipation. The holiday season is filled with festivities, parties, and traditions that provide a sense of purpose and enjoyment. People often look forward to these events and activities, and they can bring a lot of happiness and fulfillment. Once the holidays are over, individuals may find themselves feeling a sense of emptiness and boredom as they return to their regular routines. This lack of excitement and anticipation can make it difficult to find joy and motivation in everyday tasks, leading to a decrease in mood and an increased risk of depression.

Readjusting to routine after the holidays can be a challenging time for many individuals. The combination of returning to work or school, the pressure to resume daily responsibilities, and the loss of excitement and connection can all contribute to the development of depression. It is important for individuals to be mindful of their mental health during this time and to seek support if needed. By maintaining healthy relationships, establishing self-care routines, and seeking professional help if necessary, individuals can navigate the post-holiday period with greater ease and resilience.

XVII. FINDING JOY IN SIMPLE PLEASURES

Amidst the hustle and bustle of our daily lives, it can be easy to overlook the simple pleasures that bring us joy. In the essay 'Back to Routine: Depression, Relationships and Readjustment after the Holidays,' the importance of finding joy in these moments is emphasized. While the holidays are often characterized by elaborate celebrations and extravagant gifts, the real source of happiness lies in the simplicity of life. Engaging in the mundane tasks that make up our routines can surprisingly bring us immense joy and contentment. It is during these moments of routine that we can truly appreciate the beauty of the present. Whether it is sipping a cup of coffee in the morning or taking a leisurely stroll through the park, these simple acts can yield the greatest sense of happiness. In a world constantly pushing for more, it is crucial to recognize that joy can be found in the simplest of pleasures. As the essay suggests, finding contentment in these moments allows us to escape the pressures of society and rediscover the true essence of self.

Engaging in these simple pleasures can help alleviate the symptoms of depression and foster healthier relationships. Depression often emerges during times of transition, such as returning to routine after the holidays. By consciously seeking out the joy in everyday experiences, individuals can actively combat the feelings of emptiness and sadness that often accompany depression. The act of finding joy in simple pleasures can serve as a form of self-care, providing a much-needed respite from the pressures and demands of everyday life. This practice also allows for a more present and open mindset, which in turn cultivates healthier relationships with ourselves and others.

Recognizing the significance of these simple pleasures can also aid in readjustment after the holidays. As the holiday season comes to an end, it is not uncommon to experience a sense of emptiness and longing for the joyous moments that have passed. By shifting our focus towards the beauty of the present, we can ease the transition and find solace in the everyday. Embracing the mundane tasks of our routines with a renewed sense of appreciation can help fill the void left by the holiday season. The pursuit of joy in the simple pleasures of life is crucial for our overall well-being. By finding contentment in the present moment and engaging in the mundane tasks of our routines, we can experience a profound sense of happiness and connection. It is through these acts that we can combat depression, foster healthier relationships, and ease the readjustment after the holidays. It is in the simplicity of life that we can find true joy and fulfillment.

APPRECIATING SIMPLICITY

After the excitement of the holidays, finding joy in everyday moments and simple pleasures can help combat post-holiday blues. After the excitement and festivities of the holiday season come to an end, many individuals find themselves experiencing what is commonly known as the post-holiday blues. This phenomenon is characterized by feelings of sadness, restlessness, and a general sense of dissatisfaction as people transition back to their regular routines. Amidst the hustle and bustle of everyday life, there is immense value in appreciating simplicity and finding joy in everyday moments and simple pleasures. By shifting our focus from the grandeur of the holiday season to the beauty of the ordinary, we can combat these post-holiday blues and cultivate a sense of contentment and fulfillment.

Appreciating simplicity allows us to find beauty in the mundane aspects of our daily lives. It invites us to slow down and truly savor the present moment, whether that be enjoying a warm cup of coffee in the morning, taking a leisurely walk in nature, or spending quality time with loved ones. Embracing simplicity means recognizing that joy can be found in the smallest of things, and that true happiness lies in our ability to be fully present and appreciative of these moments. By reframing our perspective and seeking out these simple pleasures, we can counteract the feelings of emptiness and dissatisfaction that often accompany the post-holiday period. Finding joy in everyday moments empowers us to create our own happiness independent of external circumstances. While the holidays are often associated with extravagant gestures, material possessions, and elaborate events, the reality is that true happiness cannot be sustained through these things alone. Instead, it is found in the simple acts of kindness, the shared laughter, and the moments of connection that we experience on a daily basis. By shifting our focus away from the grandiosity of the holiday season and towards the everyday joys that surround us, we can find solace in the ordinary and combat the post-holiday blues.

Appreciating simplicity also serves as a gentle reminder to prioritize self-care and well-being. Oftentimes, the holiday season can be physically and emotionally draining, leaving us feeling depleted once it comes to an end. By embracing simplicity and finding joy in everyday moments, we are able to recharge and replenish our energy reserves. Whether it be through engaging in mindful practices such as meditation or yoga, indulging in a favorite hobby, or simply allowing ourselves time for relaxation and reflection, prioritizing self-care is essential for combating post-holiday blues and promoting overall mental, emotional, and physical well-being. As the holiday season fades and we return to our regular routines, it is crucial to appreciate simplicity and find joy in everyday moments and simple pleasures. By doing so, we can combat the post-holiday blues and foster a sense of contentment and fulfillment. Embracing the beauty of the ordinary, cultivating happiness independent of external circumstances, and prioritizing self-care are all essential strategies for navigating the transition from the excitement of the holidays to the calmness of everyday life.

ENGAGING THE SENSES

Engaging in activities that stimulate the senses, such as enjoying nature or indulging in a favorite hobby, fosters a sense of pleasure and well-being. Engaging the senses through activities that stimulate pleasure and well-being is a crucial aspect of maintaining mental health and readjusting after the holiday season. Engaging in activities such as enjoying nature or indulging in a favorite hobby can provide a much-needed sense of relief and rejuvenation. Nature has a unique ability to captivate our senses, offering a myriad of sights, sounds, smells, and even tactile experiences. Taking a leisurely stroll through a park or hiking in the mountains can awaken our visual senses and immerse us in the beauty of our surroundings. For instance, the vibrant colors of blooming flowers, the tranquility of a flowing river, or the majesty of a sunrise can evoke a sense of wonder that rejuvenates our spirits. The sounds of birds chirping, leaves rustling, or waves crashing against the shore can create a peaceful ambiance that soothes our auditory senses and helps us find solace amidst the chaos of daily life. Engaging in activities that allow us to indulge in a favorite hobby can be immensely rewarding and therapeutic. Whether it is painting, playing a musical instrument, cooking, or gardening, these activities provide us with an avenue to fully immerse ourselves and escape from the pressures of our routine. The act of creating something, be it a beautiful piece of art or a delicious meal, not only engages our senses but also instills a sense of accomplishment and satisfaction. It allows us to tap into our creative side, stimulate our minds, and Foster a sense of well-being. Engaging in such activities can also serve as a form of self-expression, helping us explore our emotions and thoughts in a safe and fulfilling manner. By incorporating activities that engage the senses into our everyday routine, we can combat the post-holiday blues and enhance our overall well-being.

Whether it is taking a leisurely bike ride, trying a new recipe, or simply taking a moment to admire a colorful sunset, these activities allow us to reconnect with ourselves and find joy in the present moment. Engaging the senses allows us to fully experience the world around us, igniting a sense of pleasure that acts as a counterbalance to the challenges and stresses of everyday life. By prioritizing these activities, we can cultivate a greater sense of pleasure and well-being, leading to improved mental health and a smoother transition back to our regular routines after the holidays.

MINDFUL APPRECIATION

Practicing gratitude for the small joys in life cultivates a positive mindset and promotes emotional resilience.

As the holiday season comes to an end and individuals return to their routines, it is essential to remember the importance of mindful appreciation. By practicing gratitude for the small joys in life, individuals can cultivate a positive mindset that contributes to their emotional resilience. Taking a moment each day to reflect on the things we are grateful for not only brings us joy but also reminds us of the abundance in our lives. It allows us to shift our perspective from focusing on what we lack to acknowledging and appreciating what we do have. This mindset of gratitude can greatly impact our overall well-being and mental health. Research has shown that practicing gratitude can lead to increased happiness, satisfaction with life, and decreased depressive symptoms. It acts as a protective factor against vulnerability to depression and helps individuals develop a more resilient mindset when facing adversity. When we consciously choose to appreciate the small joys in life, we train our minds to focus on positivity rather than dwelling on negativity or stressors. This practice helps us to reframe challenging situations and find silver linings even in difficult times. By practicing gratitude regularly, we train our brains to seek out and acknowledge positive experiences, which can enhance our overall sense of well-being. By actively cultivating a positive mindset through gratitude, we foster emotional resilience that allows us to bounce back from setbacks and adapt more effectively to stressors. Recognizing and appreciating the small joys in life can also strengthen our relationships. Expressing gratitude towards those around us not only shows our appreciation but also reinforces positive connections and fosters a sense of belonging. Gratitude cultivates empathy and encourages a positive cycle of giving and receiving. It helps us recognize the efforts and kindness of others, leading to increased feelings of gratitude and a desire to reciprocate. This can lead to more fulfilling and resilient relationships, which play a crucial role in our overall well-being. Practicing mindful appreciation by cultivating gratitude for the small joys in life has several positive effects on our mental health and relationships. It allows us to develop a positive mindset that promotes emotional resilience, helps us reframe challenging situations, and enhances our overall sense of well-being. By actively practicing gratitude, we can foster a more positive outlook on life, leading to increased happiness and satisfaction. Expressing gratitude towards others strengthens our relationships, fostering a sense of belonging and reinforcing positive connections. Making gratitude a daily practice in our routines is essential for our overall well-being and leads to a more fulfilling and resilient life. One significant aspect that individuals often struggle with after the holiday season is readjusting to their normal routines. This period of transition back to normalcy can be particularly challenging for individuals who suffer from depression. Depressive symptoms tend to worsen during the holiday season due to various stressors such as increased social pressures and expectations, financial burdens, and feelings of loneliness. The end of the holiday season does not necessarily mean an immediate alleviation of these depressive symptoms. Instead, individuals with depression often experience a post-holiday slump, making it difficult for them to return to their regular responsibilities and activities. This can further deteriorate their mood and sense of well-being, creating a vicious cycle of depression and functional impairment.

Readjusting to relationships after the holidays can also pose its own set of challenges. During the holiday season, individuals often spend an extended period of time with their loved ones, creating a sense of warmth and connection. When the holidays come to an end, people may feel a sense of separation and loneliness as they return to their daily lives. This can be especially difficult for individuals who already struggle with interpersonal relationships. The abrupt shift from holiday to routine can significantly impact the dynamics of their relationships as well. Expectations established during the holiday season, such as increased quality time or intimate moments, may not be easily maintained once the holiday spirit fades away. This can lead to feelings of disappointment, resentment, and even conflict, further exacerbating depressive symptoms. The readjustment process can be particularly arduous for college students. The holiday season often provides a much-needed break from the pressures of academic life, offering a chance for rest and relaxation. When college students return to their studies, they may face difficulties in coping with the demands of their coursework. The sudden shift from leisurely activities to academic responsibilities can be overwhelming and lead to procrastination, stress, and decreased motivation. This, in turn, can contribute to the worsening of depressive symptoms and make it even harder for students to readjust to college life. Readjusting to routine after the holiday season poses various challenges for individuals, especially those who struggle with depression. The end of the holiday season can exacerbate depressive symptoms and create a post-holiday slump that hinders functional well-being. The shift from holiday to routine can also impact the dynamics of relationships, creating a sense of separation and disappointment. College students, in particular, face additional stressors during this transition as they grapple with academic demands. It is crucial to acknowledge the difficulties associated with this period of readjustment and to provide the necessary support and resources to help individuals navigate these challenges more effectively.

XVIII.   THE ROLE OF PERSONAL REFLECTION

Personal reflection plays a crucial role in the process of readjustment after the holiday season. As individuals navigate the transition from a period of relaxation and celebration back into the routine of daily life, taking the time to reflect can offer invaluable insights and facilitate emotional and psychological well-being. Reflection allows individuals to examine their experiences, emotions, and relationships during the holiday season, providing an opportunity to gain a deeper understanding of oneself and others. This self-awareness can aid in the identification and processing of any negative emotions or stressors that may have emerged during the festivities. Personal reflection can help individuals appreciate the positive aspects of their holiday experiences, fostering a sense of gratitude and contentment. Through personal reflection, individuals can explore their emotional state and gain insight into how the holiday season has affected their overall well-being. This examination provides an opportunity to identify any signs of depression or emotional distress that may have arisen during the holidays. Recognizing these feelings is vital, as it can help individuals take appropriate action, seeking support or professional help if necessary. Personal reflection can encourage individuals to actively engage in self-care practices, such as exercise, meditation, or engaging in hobbies, to promote emotional resilience and well-being. In addition to fostering self-awareness, personal reflection allows individuals to evaluate the quality of their relationships and assess their social support systems. The holiday season often puts considerable emphasis on connections with family, friends, and loved ones. These connections may not always be positive or fulfilling. Taking the time to reflect on these relationships can help individuals discern which relationships contribute positively to their well-being and which ones may cause stress or emotional strain. Armed with this knowledge, individuals can make informed decisions about nurturing and fostering healthy relationships and setting boundaries in those that may be detrimental to their emotional well-being.

Personal reflection can enhance an individual's ability to manage stress and readjust to the demands of daily life after the holiday season. By reflecting on the holiday experiences, individuals can identify stressors or triggers that caused them distress during this time. Armed with this knowledge, individuals can formulate coping strategies or establish healthy boundaries to mitigate or navigate these stressors effectively. Such self-reflection can also serve as a springboard for setting realistic goals and developing action plans for personal and professional endeavors in the coming months. Personal reflection is a vital tool in the process of readjustment after the holiday season. By examining their experiences, emotions, and relationships, individuals can gain valuable insights into their well-being, address any negative emotions, and appreciate the positive aspects of their holiday experiences. Through personal reflection, individuals can foster self-awareness, evaluate their relationships, manage stress, and set goals for personal and professional growth. As individuals transition back into their routine, personal reflection serves as a guide for navigating the complexities of

post-holiday life and promoting overall emotional and psychological well-being.

REFLECTING ON THE HOLIDAY SEASON

Taking time to reflect on personal experiences during the holidays enables individuals to process emotions and learn from past events. Reflecting on the holiday season can be an important practice for individuals to process their emotions and learn from past experiences. The holiday season is often a time filled with a mix of joy and stress, as individuals navigate family gatherings, gift-giving, and other traditions. By taking the time to reflect on these experiences, individuals can better understand and process the range of emotions they felt during this time, whether it be happiness, sadness, or even frustration. Self-reflection allows individuals to explore the root causes of these emotions and identify any patterns or triggers that may have contributed to their experiences during the holidays.

Reflecting on personal experiences during the holidays can offer valuable lessons and opportunities for growth. By examining past events, individuals can gain insights into their own behaviors and reactions. They can identify areas where they may have succeeded, such as maintaining healthy boundaries with family or finding meaningful ways to give back to their community. Likewise, they can also recognize areas for improvement, such as finding healthier coping mechanisms for holiday stress or addressing conflicts with loved ones. Reflecting on personal experiences during the holiday season can provide individuals with a greater sense of self-awareness. It allows individuals to recognize their own emotional triggers, which is essential for managing their mental and emotional well-being. Through reflection, individuals may identify patterns of behavior or thought that contributed to negative experiences during the holidays. This self-awareness can empower individuals to make conscious choices and take proactive steps to address these triggers in future holiday seasons. Taking the time to reflect on personal experiences during the holidays can also facilitate the process of readjustment and transitioning back to the routine after the holiday season has ended. By reflecting on the highs and lows of the holiday season, individuals can gain a sense of closure and find a renewed sense of purpose as they move forward. This reflection can provide individuals with a clearer perspective on their goals and priorities, enabling them to set realistic expectations and make positive changes in their lives.

Reflection on personal experiences during the holiday season is an important practice for individuals to process emotions and learn from past events. It allows individuals to gain insights into their emotions, behaviors, and triggers, facilitating personal growth and self-awareness. Reflection aids in the process of readjustment, helping individuals to transition back to their routines with a greater sense of purpose and clarity. By taking the time to reflect, individuals can make the most of the holiday season and find meaning in the experiences they have had.

IDENTIFYING STRENGTHS AND AREAS FOR GROWTH

Reflective practices help individuals recognize personal strengths, as well as areas in which they can grow and improve. Identifying strengths and areas for growth is an essential aspect of personal development, and reflective practices play a crucial role in this process. Through introspection and careful examination of experiences, individuals are able to recognize their personal strengths and abilities. Reflective practices provide an opportunity for individuals to acknowledge and celebrate their accomplishments, building self-confidence and self-esteem. By reflecting on past successes and achievements, individuals can develop a clearer understanding of their unique strengths and talents, which can be further leveraged in various aspects of their lives. Reflective practices also help individuals identify areas in which they can grow and improve. By critically analyzing their experiences and actions, individuals gain insight into their weaknesses and shortcomings. This self-awareness is a crucial step towards personal growth, as it allows individuals to identify areas in which they need to develop and improve. Reflective practices enable individuals to view challenges and failures not as roadblocks, but as opportunities for growth and learning. By acknowledging their areas for improvement, individuals can take proactive steps towards personal development, seeking out resources and strategies that can help them overcome their limitations. Reflective practices empower individuals to lead a more meaningful and fulfilling life, as it encourages them to continuously strive for self-improvement. The process of reflection is particularly pertinent during the post-holiday period when individuals may experience a range of emotions, such as depression, relationship strain, and difficulty readjusting to their routine. Reflecting on these challenges can provide individuals with valuable insights into their emotional well-being, as well as the dynamics of their relationships. This self-reflection can help individuals identify the underlying causes of their emotional distress or relationship difficulties and take appropriate measures to address them. Reflection can also provide individuals with a better understanding of the impact that the holiday period has had on their mood and well-being. Armed with this knowledge, individuals can then develop effective coping strategies to manage their emotions and relationships better. Reflective practices play a crucial role in helping individuals identify their personal strengths and areas for growth. By engaging in introspection and critical analysis, individuals can celebrate their accomplishments and develop self-confidence, while also recognizing their weaknesses and taking proactive steps towards personal development. This process of reflection is particularly relevant during the post-holiday period, as it enables individuals to gain insights into their emotional well-being and relationships, leading to a more meaningful and fulfilling life.

SETTING INTENTIONS

Utilizing insights gained from reflection, individuals can set intentions for personal development and positive change in the post-holiday period. Setting intentions is a crucial step in personal development and positive change, especially in the post-holiday period. Reflection allows individuals to gain valuable insights into their experiences over the holiday season, enabling them to identify areas for improvement and growth. By consciously setting intentions, individuals can take deliberate actions towards achieving their desired outcomes. For example, someone who realized that they had neglected their physical health during the holidays may set an intention to prioritize regular exercise and healthy eating. They can then create a plan of action, such as scheduling regular workout sessions and preparing nutritious meals in advance. By setting these intentions and following through on their plan, individuals can foster positive change in their lifestyle and well-being. In addition to personal development, setting intentions can also contribute to improving relationships. Reflection allows individuals to recognize any negative patterns or behaviors they may have engaged in during the holidays, such as being overly critical or neglecting quality time with loved ones. Armed with this awareness, individuals can set intentions to cultivate healthier and more fulfilling relationships. This may involve committing to better communication, spending quality time together, or expressing gratitude and appreciation more frequently. By setting intentions to prioritize and nurture their relationships, individuals can strengthen their bonds and create a more positive and harmonious environment for themselves and those around them.

Setting intentions also helps individuals readjust to the routine after the holidays. The transition from a relaxed and festive period back to the demands of work and daily responsibilities can be challenging. By setting intentions, individuals can approach this readjustment with a positive mindset and clear goals. For example, someone who struggled with procrastination during the holidays may set an intention to be more organized and focused in their work. They can create a plan to establish a daily routine, set achievable goals, and break tasks into manageable steps. By setting these intentions, individuals can regain a sense of control and motivation, making the readjustment process smoother and more productive. Setting intentions based on insights gained from reflection is essential for personal development and positive change in the post-holiday period. By consciously setting intentions, individuals can take deliberate actions to achieve their desired outcomes, whether it be improving their well-being, strengthening relationships, or readjusting to the routine. Through reflection and intentional goal-setting, individuals can pave the way for a fulfilling and successful post-holiday period. After the hustle and bustle of the holiday season comes to an end, many people find themselves experiencing a wide range of emotions as they transition back to their normal routines. For some, this post-holiday period can be particularly challenging, as they struggle with feelings of depression and anxiety. The holidays are often seen as a time of joy and celebration, so when the festivities come to a close, it can feel like a sudden and sharp contrast to the happiness that was once present. This transition can be especially difficult for those who have experienced loss or have strained relationships with their loved ones, as the holiday season often puts a great deal of emphasis on family and togetherness.

The pressure to be happy and cheerful during this time can be overwhelming for those who are already struggling with depression. The sudden shift from constant engagement and socializing to a more isolated and routine-based lifestyle can exacerbate these feelings, as individuals may find themselves feeling disconnected and lonely. This isolation can be even more pronounced for those who do not have a support system or a strong network of friends. The post-holiday period can feel like a void, as individuals navigate their way back to a life that may seem mundane in comparison to the excitement of the holidays. Strained or broken relationships can also contribute to feelings of depression and anxiety during this time. The holidays often bring people together, and it is during this time when individuals may be faced with unresolved conflicts or unfulfilled expectations in their relationships. The pressure to maintain a cheerful facade can make it difficult for individuals to confront these issues head-on, leaving them feeling frustrated and unfulfilled. As the holidays fade away, these unresolved conflicts can resurface and amplify feelings of sadness and loneliness.

To readjust to routine after the holidays, it is important for individuals to acknowledge and address their feelings. This may involve seeking professional help, whether that be through therapy or counseling. Talking to a trained professional can provide valuable insights and coping strategies for navigating the post-holiday period. Reaching out to friends or loved ones can also be beneficial, as they can offer a support system and a listening ear during this time. Engaging in self-care activities such as exercise, practicing Mindfulness , and maintaining a healthy lifestyle can also help individuals manage their emotions and readjust to their routine in a positive way.

The post-holiday period can be a challenging time for many individuals, especially those who struggle with depression and strained relationships. The sudden shift from the excitement and togetherness of the holidays to a more isolated and routine-based lifestyle can exacerbate feelings of sadness and loneliness. By acknowledging and addressing these feelings, seeking professional help if necessary, and engaging in self-care activities, individuals can navigate this transition and readjust to their routine in a healthy and positive way.

XIX. LEARNING FROM HOLIDAY EXPERIENCES

As the holiday season comes to an end and we gradually settle back into our routines, it is essential to reflect on the experiences we had and the lessons we can learn from them. The holiday period is often filled with joy and excitement, but it can also bring about a range of emotions, including depression, strain on relationships, and difficulty readjusting to daily life afterward. One important lesson we can glean from our holiday experiences is the importance of self-care and mental health. Throughout the festivities, it is common for individuals to neglect their own well-being while prioritizing the needs and expectations of others. This neglect can lead to feelings of depression and a sense of being overwhelmed, especially when the holiday season comes to an end and the support and activities that came along with it dissipate. Another valuable lesson that our holiday experiences teach us is the significance of maintaining healthy relationships. The holiday period is often a time when families and friends come together to celebrate and share quality time. It is also a time when disagreements and conflicts can arise, as different personalities and expectations clash. Reflecting on these experiences can help individuals gain a deeper understanding of their own behavior and the dynamics within their relationships. By recognizing and addressing any issues that emerged during the holidays, individuals can work towards building stronger and more harmonious relationships moving forward.

Readjusting to daily life after a period of excitement and festivities can be challenging for many individuals. The abrupt shift from a relaxed and carefree attitude to the demands and pressures of daily responsibilities can lead to feelings of anxiety and stress. This readjustment presents an opportunity for personal growth and resilience. By reflecting on the experience of transitioning back to routine, individuals can identify strategies that worked well and those that did not. This self-reflection can pave the way for effective coping mechanisms and the development of a mindset that embraces change and adapts to new situations. The holiday period offers a wealth of experiences that we can learn from to improve our well-being, relationships, and ability to adapt. Taking the time to reflect on the emotional highs and lows of the holidays can provide insight into our own needs, the dynamics within our relationships, and the strategies that can aid in readjustment. By incorporating these lessons into our daily lives, we can foster personal growth and resilience while maintaining a healthy and fulfilling lifestyle outside of the holiday season. It is crucial to approach the end of the holiday period as an opportunity for reflection, self-improvement, and a renewed focus on our mental and emotional well-being.

LESSONS FROM CHALLENGES

Examining challenges faced during the holiday season provides opportunities for personal growth and improvement in future interactions. Examining challenges faced during the holiday season provides opportunities for personal growth and improvement in future interactions. The holiday season can be a particularly challenging time for many individuals, as it often magnifies feelings of loneliness, depression, and anxiety. The pressure to conform to societal expectations of joy and togetherness can be overwhelming, leading to feelings of inadequacy or disappointment for those who may not have the same experience. It is through these challenges that individuals can gain a deeper understanding of themselves and their relationships. For instance, the holiday season may bring to light the importance of setting boundaries and communicating effectively with loved ones. As individuals navigate spending time with various family members and friends, conflicts or disagreements may arise. These disagreements can provide an opportunity for growth by highlighting areas where personal boundaries may have been violated or communication breakdowns occurred.

Through reflection and understanding, individuals can learn to better assert their needs and expectations in future interactions. The challenges faced during the holiday season can also shed light on the importance of self-care and mental well-being. The pressures of the holiday season can often lead to neglecting one's own needs in favor of pleasing others or meeting societal expectations. It is crucial to prioritize self-care and mental well-being in order to maintain healthy relationships and personal growth. Taking the time to nurture one's own mental health can lead to increased self-awareness, improved emotional resilience, and better overall functioning. The challenges faced during the holiday season can also serve as a catalyst for personal growth and change. For many, the holiday season marks a time of reflection and evaluation of personal goals, values, and priorities. It is during this time that individuals may reassess their relationships, career aspirations, and personal growth trajectories. The challenges faced can serve as a reminder to make positive changes and take steps towards a more fulfilling and meaningful life. Examining the challenges faced during the holiday season can provide valuable lessons for personal growth and improvement in future interactions. From setting boundaries and communicating effectively to prioritizing self-care and reassessing personal goals, individuals can use these challenges as opportunities to learn, grow, and better understand themselves and their relationships. By taking the time to reflect and make positive changes, individuals can navigate future interactions with increased self-awareness, emotional resilience, and a deeper understanding of their own needs and priorities.

BUILDING RESILIENCE

Analyzing coping strategies and seeking lessons from difficult experiences fosters resilience, allowing for better management of post-holiday stressors. Building resilience is a crucial component in effectively managing post-holiday stressors. Resilience refers to the ability to bounce back and recover from difficult experiences, and it can be developed through various coping strategies and the examination of lessons learned from past challenges. Coping strategies such as seeking social support, engaging in self-care activities, and practicing Mindfulness can significantly contribute to building resilience and improving overall well-being. By reaching out to friends, family, or support groups, individuals can gain the emotional support and guidance necessary to navigate through stressful periods. This social support network acts as a safety net, providing a sense of belonging and stabilizing one's emotional state. Self-care activities, such as exercising, eating well, and getting enough sleep, also play a vital role in building resilience. Engaging in these activities enhances physical and mental well-being, enabling individuals to better withstand stress and effectively manage their emotions. Practicing Mindfulness , such as meditation or deep breathing exercises, can help individuals develop the ability to stay present and focused, effectively reducing anxiety and promoting a sense of calm. Analyzing past difficult experiences and seeking lessons from them is another important aspect of building resilience. Reflection allows individuals to gain insights into their own coping mechanisms and identify areas for growth and improvement. By understanding what worked and what didn't in the past, individuals can develop a more effective toolkit of strategies to cope with future stressors. Examining past challenges can provide valuable lessons about personal strengths and weaknesses, promoting a sense of self-awareness and strengthening one's ability to face adversity. This reflection can be facilitated through journaling, therapy, or engaging in conversations with trusted individuals who can provide objective perspectives and guidance.

Building resilience is essential for effectively managing post-holiday stressors. Coping strategies such as seeking social support, engaging in self-care activities, and practicing Mindfulness contribute to fostering resilience and improving overall well-being. Analyzing past difficult experiences and seeking lessons from them helps individuals develop a more effective toolkit of coping strategies, promoting personal growth and self-awareness. By prioritizing resilience-building practices, individuals can navigate through challenges more effectively and maintain their mental and emotional well-being in the face of post-holiday stressors.

APPLYING KNOWLEDGE MOVING FORWARD

Applying lessons learned to future holiday seasons empowers individuals to approach subsequent holidays with greater emotional preparedness and adaptability.

As the holiday season comes to an end, individuals have the opportunity to reflect on their experiences and apply the knowledge gained to future holiday seasons. Taking the time to assess what worked well and what did not can empower individuals to approach subsequent holidays with greater emotional preparedness and adaptability. By reflecting on past holiday experiences, individuals can better understand their own emotions and triggers, allowing them to make necessary adjustments moving forward. For example, if someone felt overwhelmed by the number of social commitments during the holidays, they can implement strategies such as prioritizing events, setting boundaries, and practicing self-care to alleviate stress in the future. Applying the lessons learned from past holiday experiences can improve relationships with loved ones. By reflecting on how interactions and dynamics played out during the holidays, individuals can gain insights into their communication patterns and areas for growth. This knowledge can be used to enhance future interactions and foster stronger connections with family and friends. Applying lessons learned can also help individuals to manage expectations during the holidays. It is common for individuals to have high expectations for this time of year, leading to disappointment when reality does not measure up to their visions. By reflecting on past experiences, individuals can identify unrealistic expectations and adopt a more realistic mindset, allowing them to embrace the imperfect nature of holiday celebrations. This shift in perspective can reduce stress and frustration, promoting a more enjoyable holiday experience. Applying knowledge moving forward can foster a greater sense of adaptability during the holidays. Life is constantly changing, and what may have worked well in previous years may not be suitable in the present. By acknowledging this, individuals can embrace flexibility and adapt their traditions and routines to fit their current circumstances. For instance, if someone has recently experienced a loss or significant life change, they may need to adjust their holiday plans or create new traditions to accommodate their emotional needs. By doing so, individuals can navigate the holiday season with greater ease and resilience. Applying lessons learned to future holiday seasons is essential for emotional preparedness and adaptability. Reflecting on past experiences allows individuals to gain insights into their emotions, relationships, expectations, and adaptability. Armed with this knowledge, individuals can make necessary adjustments, strengthen their relationships, manage expectations, and embrace adaptability during subsequent holiday seasons. By doing so, individuals can cultivate a more fulfilling and enjoyable holiday experience for themselves and those around them. Depression is a complex mental health condition that affects millions of people worldwide. While it can arise at any time, the holiday season is often particularly challenging for individuals struggling with depression. The pressure to be joyful and surrounded by loved ones can intensify feelings of loneliness and isolation, leading to a worsening of depressive symptoms. The disruption of routine during the holidays can also contribute to feelings of anxiety and sadness. After the holidays, individuals may find it difficult to readjust to their regular lives, especially in the context of relationships. Maintaining healthy relationships requires effort and communication, and the holiday season often disrupts these dynamics. The expectation of constant togetherness during the holidays can lead to feelings of suffocation and tension within relationships. Consequently, when the holiday season ends, couples and families may struggle to establish a new routine that fosters a balance between spending quality time together and maintaining personal space. The financial strain associated with holiday expenses can also create conflict and tension within relationships, as financial stress has been found to be a significant predictor of relationship dissatisfaction. The end of the holiday season can bring with it a need to renegotiate financial expectations and set realistic goals for the future. Beyond relationships, readjusting to routine after the holidays can be challenging for individuals with depression. The abrupt shift from holiday cheer and leisure to work or school responsibilities can be overwhelming and contribute to a dip in mood. Individuals may feel a sense of emptiness or loss after the festivities, as the anticipation and excitement of the holiday season fades away. It is crucial for individuals to acknowledge these feelings and prioritize self-care during this readjustment period. Establishing a routine that incorporates activities and behaviors that bring joy and fulfillment, such as exercise, hobbies, and socializing, can help combat post-holiday blues and promote overall well-being. The period following the holidays can be challenging for individuals struggling with depression, as the disruption of routine and the pressure associated with relationships can exacerbate symptoms. By acknowledging and addressing these challenges, individuals can take steps towards readjustment and prioritize their mental health and well-being.

XX. PROMOTING A SUPPORTIVE ENVIRONMENT

Promoting a supportive environment is crucial in facilitating the process of readjustment after the holiday season. A supportive environment can provide individuals with the necessary resources and tools to cope with post-holiday depression and maintain healthy relationships. In this regard, one effective strategy is to establish support groups or workshops where individuals can come together and share their experiences. These groups can serve as a safe space for individuals to express their feelings, seek advice, and receive emotional support from others who are going through similar challenges. These groups can also provide a platform for individuals to learn coping mechanisms and strategies from one another, which can significantly contribute to their overall well-being. Fostering a supportive environment can also be achieved by promoting open communication and empathy within relationships.

This can involve encouraging individuals to express their emotions and concerns to their loved ones and creating a space where such conversations are welcomed and validated. By doing so, individuals can feel heard and understood, and it can also pave the way for problem-solving and conflict resolution if necessary. Practicing empathy and actively listening to others' experiences can further enhance the quality of relationships and contribute to a sense of belonging and validation.

Another important aspect of promoting a supportive environment is recognizing and addressing any stigmas or misconceptions surrounding post-holiday depression and readjustment. Often, individuals may feel ashamed or embarrassed to seek help or discuss their struggles due to societal expectations or perceived judgments. It is crucial to engage in educational campaigns or initiatives aimed at raising awareness and increasing understanding about post-holiday depression. These efforts can include sharing personal stories, organizing workshops on mental health, or disseminating information through various media platforms. By doing so, individuals can feel more comfortable and supported in seeking help and discussing their experiences without fear of judgment. Reducing stigmas and promoting a supportive environment can improve overall mental health and well-being as individuals are more likely to seek timely assistance and adopt healthier coping strategies.

Creating a supportive environment is essential in facilitating the process of readjustment after the holiday season. Through support groups, open communication, empathy, and addressing stigmas, individuals can receive emotional support, learn coping mechanisms, and maintain healthy relationships. By promoting a supportive environment, individuals can navigate the challenges of post-holiday depression more effectively, fostering overall well-being and ensuring a smoother transition to the routine of everyday life. In doing so, individuals can find solace and understanding within their communities, strengthening their resilience and ability to thrive in the face of adversity.

OPEN COMMUNICATION

Creating an environment where individuals feel comfortable expressing their post-holiday struggles builds a support network. Open communication is a crucial component in creating an environment where individuals feel comfortable expressing their post-holiday struggles. After the joy and excitement of the holiday season, many individuals find themselves grappling with a range of emotions, including sadness, stress, and a sense of emptiness. By fostering an atmosphere of open communication, individuals are more likely to reach out for support and are less likely to feel isolated in their struggles. When individuals feel safe to share their post-holiday struggles, it not only allows them to vent their feelings but also helps build a support network. This support network can consist of friends, family, or even mental health professionals who can provide guidance and reassurance during this challenging time. By creating an environment where individuals feel comfortable expressing their emotions, it becomes easier for them to acknowledge and work through their post-holiday struggles. Open communication allows individuals to gain a better understanding of their own emotions and experiences. Often, people may not even be aware of the extent of their post-holiday struggles until they articulate them. By openly discussing their feelings, individuals can gain perspective on the underlying causes of their emotional distress. This self-reflection can be a catalyst for personal growth and can help individuals identify any patterns or triggers that may be contributing to their post-holiday struggle. Through open communication, individuals can learn from others who may have faced similar challenges and have found effective coping strategies. In addition to fostering personal growth, open communication also strengthens relationships. When individuals feel comfortable expressing their struggles to their loved ones, it deepens the level of trust and intimacy in those relationships. This trust allows for more meaningful connections and can lead to greater emotional support. Open communication promotes empathy and understanding among individuals. It helps create an atmosphere of mutual support where people are willing to listen and offer assistance to others who may be experiencing post-holiday difficulties. This sense of shared support not only alleviates the burden on the individual struggling but also reinforces a sense of community. Open communication plays a vital role in creating an environment where individuals feel comfortable expressing their post-holiday struggles. By fostering an atmosphere of open dialogue, individuals are more likely to reach out for support, gain a better understanding of their emotions, and strengthen their relationships. Building a support network through open communication can provide crucial guidance and reassurance during the challenging time of readjustment after the holidays. Open communication promotes personal growth and allows individuals to learn from others who have faced similar challenges. Open communication helps individuals acknowledge, process, and work through their post-holiday struggles in a healthy and supportive way.

MUTUAL UNDERSTANDING

Encouraging empathy and understanding among friends, family, and colleagues promotes a sense of belonging and validation.

As individuals navigate the complexities of life, it is vital to foster mutual understanding in our relationships to establish a sense of belonging and validation. Developing empathy allows us to connect with others on a deeper level, as we strive to understand their experiences and emotions. By actively listening and seeking to comprehend their perspectives, we create an environment of support and acceptance, fostering healthy relationships. Within the realm of family dynamics, promoting empathy and understanding helps build strong bonds and a sense of shared experiences. When family members make an effort to understand one another's perspectives, conflicts can be resolved more effectively, allowing for a harmonious atmosphere within the family unit. Similarly, empathy and understanding play a crucial role in friendships. Friends who are understanding and empathetic create a safe space where individuals can express themselves without fear of judgment or rejection. This validation contributes to a sense of belonging, allowing individuals to feel accepted and appreciated in their friendships. Fostering empathy and understanding among colleagues can have a positive impact on workplace dynamics. Encouraging empathy promotes a supportive work environment, where colleagues are more willing to collaborate and assist one another. By understanding and considering the unique perspectives and experiences of co-workers, teams can work more harmoniously, leading to increased productivity and job satisfaction. Mutual understanding also plays a pivotal role in the readjustment process after the holiday season. The transition from a more relaxed holiday routine back to the demands of everyday life can be challenging, often leading to feelings of depression and anxiety. By encouraging empathy and understanding in our relationships, we can navigate this readjustment period with greater ease. Being understanding and empathetic towards our own emotions and those of others allows us to acknowledge and address any difficult feelings that arise. This understanding can lead to a validation of our experiences, easing the readjustment process. Fostering mutual understanding is crucial in cultivating a sense of belonging and validation in our relationships. By promoting empathy and understanding among friends, family, and colleagues, we create supportive environments where individuals can express themselves freely. This understanding contributes to stronger family bonds, more fulfilling friendships, and a more harmonious workplace. Mutual understanding plays a vital role in the readjustment process after the holiday season, helping individuals navigate the challenges of returning to routine. By prioritizing empathy and understanding, we can build stronger connections and promote emotional well-being within our relationships.

OFFERING ENCOURAGEMENT

Providing encouragement and support to those facing post-holiday challenges contributes to their overall well-being and readjustment. Offering encouragement and support to individuals who are facing post-holiday challenges is crucial in promoting their overall well-being and readjustment. The holiday season often brings about a sense of joy and excitement, but it can also leave individuals feeling overwhelmed and emotionally drained once it is over. This can be particularly challenging for individuals who struggle with mental health issues such as depression or anxiety. By offering encouragement, we are giving them a sense of hope and motivation to navigate through this challenging time. One way to offer encouragement is by acknowledging the challenges they may be facing and empathizing with their feelings. Letting them know that they are not alone in their struggles can provide a sense of validation and support. Understanding that post-holiday blues are a common experience for many individuals can help them feel less isolated and more connected to others. Expressing empathy towards their emotions shows that we genuinely care about their well-being, which can be incredibly empowering.

Another way to offer encouragement is by reminding them of their strengths and past achievements. By highlighting their resilience and ability to overcome previous challenges, we can instill a sense of self-confidence and motivation. Reminding them of the skills and coping mechanisms they have developed can empower them to tackle the post-holiday challenges head-on. Discussing their previous successes can help shift their focus from the present difficulties to the potential for future growth and happiness. Providing tangible support is also an essential aspect of offering encouragement during this time. This can include offering to help them with specific tasks or responsibilities that may feel overwhelming. By assisting them with practical matters, such as organizing their schedule or helping them with household chores, we alleviate some of their stress and provide a sense of relief. This type of support can be particularly valuable for individuals who may be feeling physically and emotionally drained after the holiday season. Offering encouragement involves creating a safe and non-judgmental space for individuals to express their feelings. By actively listening and validating their emotions, we create an environment that promotes open and honest communication. This allows individuals to freely express their concerns and challenges, which can ultimately lead to a greater sense of self-awareness and emotional well-being. Offering encouragement and support to those facing post-holiday challenges contributes significantly to their overall well-being and readjustment. By empathizing with their feelings, reminding them of their strengths, providing tangible support, and creating a safe space for expression, we can empower individuals to navigate through this difficult period. Encouragement plays a pivotal role in helping individuals recover from the post-holiday blues and regain a sense of stability and happiness in their lives. As the holiday season comes to an end, many individuals find themselves having mixed emotions about returning to their daily routines. This transition from the joy and excitement of the holidays to the normalcy of everyday life can often lead to feelings of depression and sadness. The holiday season is a time when people come together, celebrate, and create memories with loved ones. Once the decorations are put away and the festivities are over, it can be difficult to adjust to the solitude and lack of companionship that is often associated with returning to routine. This readjustment period can be particularly challenging for individuals who struggle with depression, as the holiday season provides a temporary reprieve from their symptoms. For these individuals, the return to routine can feel overwhelming, leading to feelings of hopelessness and despair. In addition to the emotional toll that the end of the holiday season can take on individuals with depression, it can also impact their relationships. During the holidays, people often spend a significant amount of time with family and friends, creating a sense of togetherness and connection. Unfortunately, once the holidays are over, it can be difficult to maintain these relationships, as everyone goes back to their respective daily lives and responsibilities. This can leave individuals with depression feeling isolated and alone, as they struggle to find the same level of support and companionship they experienced during the holiday season. Readjusting to routine after the holidays can be a daunting task for anyone, regardless of whether they struggle with depression or not. The abrupt end to the festivities and the return to work or school can bring about feelings of uncertainty, stress, and fatigue. It may take some time for individuals to get back into the swing of things and find their rhythm once again. This process can be particularly challenging for those who have had a long break, as it can be difficult to regain focus and motivation after an extended period of relaxation.

The end of the holiday season often brings with it a range of emotions and challenges. For individuals with depression, returning to routine can trigger feelings of depression and sadness as the temporary reprieve from symptoms comes to an end. The readjustment period can be particularly challenging as it often leads to a sense of isolation and loneliness, as individuals try to rebuild relationships that were nurtured during the holiday season. Readjusting to routine after the holidays can be a daunting task for anyone, as it requires re-establishing focus and motivation. It is important for individuals to be mindful of these challenges and to take care of their mental health as they navigate this potentially difficult period of readjustment.

XXI. SEEKING PROFESSIONAL GUIDANCE

In our modern society, seeking professional guidance has become increasingly important in the pursuit of mental well-being. The twenty-first century has brought about numerous challenges that can greatly impact an individual's mental health, such as the fast-paced nature of daily life, overwhelming workloads, and the constant exposure to technology and social media. As a result, individuals may find themselves feeling overwhelmed, anxious, or even depressed, especially after returning to their regular routines following the holidays. It is during these times of readjustment that seeking professional guidance proves to be crucial in alleviating the effects of depression and maintaining healthy relationships. Depression, often characterized by persistent feelings of sadness, hopelessness, and a lack of interest in previously enjoyable activities, can take a toll on one's overall well-being. The return to routine after a period of relaxation and holiday cheer can exacerbate these feelings, making it difficult to find motivation and joy in daily life. Seeking professional guidance provides individuals with access to therapists, counselors, and psychologists who are trained to address and treat depression. Through various therapeutic techniques, such as cognitive-behavioral therapy or psychodynamic therapy, individuals can learn coping mechanisms, gain insight into their thought patterns, and develop strategies to overcome depressive symptoms. These professionals can provide guidance and support as individuals navigate the challenges of readjustment, helping them regain their sense of self and find meaning and fulfillment in their daily lives.

Seeking professional guidance is also essential for maintaining healthy relationships. Returning to routine after the holidays can cause strain on interpersonal connections, whether it be with romantic partners, family members, or friends. The holiday season often provides a respite from the stressors of everyday life, allowing individuals to reconnect with loved ones and foster meaningful connections. The return to the demands of work, school, and other responsibilities can lead to neglecting these relationships. Seeking the help of a professional can assist individuals in better understanding their communication styles, resolving conflicts, and enhancing their emotional intelligence. By addressing relationship challenges head-on, individuals can ensure the longevity and well-being of their connections, ultimately leading to more fulfilling and healthier bonds.

The twenty-first century has ushered in a multitude of challenges that can greatly impact an individual's mental health and well-being. The return to routine after the holidays can heighten feelings of depression and strain interpersonal relationships. Seeking professional guidance is crucial in addressing these challenges. Through therapy, individuals can learn coping mechanisms to combat depression and regain their sense of joy and fulfillment. Likewise, professional guidance can help individuals navigate the difficulties of maintaining healthy relationships, ensuring the longevity and strength of these connections. In an age where mental health is increasingly prioritized, seeking professional guidance proves to be an essential step towards achieving overall well-being and happiness.

RECOGNIZING WHEN TO SEEK HELP

Knowing when post-holiday challenges are overwhelming and beyond personal coping strategies is crucial for seeking professional support. Recognizing when to seek help: Knowing when post-holiday challenges are overwhelming and beyond personal coping strategies is crucial for seeking professional support. The holiday season often brings joy and excitement, but it can also leave individuals feeling emotionally drained and overwhelmed. As the festivities come to an end and the reality of returning to routine sets in, many people may find themselves struggling to adjust to their daily lives. This readjustment period can be particularly challenging for individuals who already experience symptoms of depression. The sudden change in routine, along with the added stress of school or work, can exacerbate feelings of sadness and hopelessness. It is essential for individuals in this situation to recognize when their coping strategies are no longer sufficient and professional support is necessary.

One sign that post-holiday challenges may be overwhelming is a persistent feeling of sadness or emptiness. While it is common to feel a bit down after the holiday season, this should not persist for an extended period of time. If a person finds themselves unable to shake off these negative emotions, even after resuming their normal routine, it may be an indication that they need additional help. Another red flag to watch out for is a loss of interest or pleasure in activities that used to bring joy. If someone finds themselves no longer enjoying activities they used to love before the holidays, it may be a sign of depression and should not be ignored. Changes in sleeping and eating patterns can also indicate that post-holiday challenges have become overwhelming. Difficulty falling asleep, frequent awakenings during the night, or excessive sleeping, can all be signs of depression. Similarly, an increase or decrease in appetite can also be indicators that a person's coping mechanisms are no longer effective. If these changes persist for longer than a few weeks, it is crucial to seek professional support for appropriate intervention. Difficulty in maintaining relationships can be a clear sign that post-holiday challenges have become overwhelming. Depression often affects individuals' ability to connect with others and can lead to feelings of isolation and withdrawal. If someone finds themselves consistently struggling to engage in social interactions or experiencing strained relationships with loved ones, seeking professional support may be beneficial in improving relationship dynamics and reducing feelings of loneliness. Recognizing when to seek help is paramount when post-holiday challenges become overwhelming and beyond personal coping strategies. Persistent feelings of sadness, loss of interest in activities, changes in sleep and eating patterns, and difficulties in maintaining relationships are all signs that additional support may be necessary. It is essential to understand that seeking professional help is not a sign of weakness, but rather a proactive step towards better mental health and well-being. By reaching out to qualified professionals, individuals can access the necessary tools and strategies to navigate the challenges that arise after the holiday season and find solace and joy in their everyday lives.

THERAPEUTIC INTERVENTIONS

Psychotherapy, counseling, and support groups can offer guidance and coping strategies tailored to individual needs.
Therapeutic interventions such as psychotherapy, counseling, and support groups are valuable resources that can provide guidance and coping strategies specifically tailored to individual needs. The post-holiday period can be particularly challenging for those who suffer from depression and have difficulty readjusting to their regular routines. Psychotherapy, also known as talk therapy, is an evidence-based approach that involves discussions between a therapist and a patient. It aims to identify and address the underlying causes of depression, teaching the patient effective coping mechanisms, and providing them with the necessary tools to manage their symptoms. With the guidance of a trained therapist, individuals can explore their feelings, thoughts, and behaviors in a safe and supportive environment, working towards developing healthier ways of thinking and behaving. Counseling is another therapeutic intervention that focuses on emotional support and guidance. Professional counselors provide a space where individuals can express their concerns, fears, and struggles without judgment. They offer a listening ear, empathy, and practical advice to help their clients navigate through post-holiday depression and readjust to their daily lives. By actively engaging in counseling sessions, individuals are encouraged to explore their emotions and gain insight into their difficulties, thus enabling them to identify and implement coping strategies that are suitable for their specific needs. Support groups are also a valuable therapeutic intervention for

individuals struggling with post-holiday depression. These groups provide a safe and inclusive space for individuals to connect and share their experiences with others who are facing similar challenges. By participating in support groups, individuals can gain a sense of validation, belonging, and understanding. They can also learn from others' experiences and collective wisdom, as well as receive practical advice and coping strategies from those who have successfully managed their post-holiday depression. Support groups offer a unique opportunity for individuals to build a support network, enhance their social connections, and reduce feelings of isolation and loneliness.

Therapeutic interventions such as psychotherapy, counseling, and support groups play a vital role in providing much-needed guidance and coping strategies for individuals struggling with post-holiday depression. The tailored approach offered in psychotherapy helps individuals identify and address the underlying causes of their depression, while counseling provides emotional support and practical advice specific to their needs. Support groups, on the other hand, offer a sense of validation, understanding, and connection with others facing similar challenges. By engaging in these therapeutic interventions, individuals can acquire the necessary tools to navigate through their post-holiday depression and successfully readjust to their regular routines.

BUILDING A SUPPORT TEAM

Collaborating with mental health professionals and creating a network of support enhances the readjustment process after the holiday season. The holiday season is often portrayed as a time of joy and celebration, but for many individuals, it can also be a source of stress and anxiety. The expectation of happiness and togetherness can intensify feelings of loneliness or sadness, especially for those who have experienced loss or are grappling with issues such as depression. There are strategies that can help navigate the post-holiday readjustment period and create a support system that enhances well-being. Collaborating with mental health professionals is one key component of building a support team. These professionals have the knowledge and expertise to provide guidance and support during the readjustment process. They can help individuals identify coping mechanisms, manage stress, and develop healthier ways of dealing with negative emotions. Mental health professionals can also provide therapy and counseling services, which can be beneficial for those who need a safe space to express their feelings and work through any challenges they may be experiencing. Alongside working with mental health professionals, creating a network of support is equally vital. This network can include friends, family members, and other individuals who can offer emotional support, understanding, and encouragement. Sharing experiences, emotions, and struggles with trusted individuals can alleviate feelings of isolation and provide a sense of belonging. These individuals can help with practical matters such as providing assistance with household tasks, running errands, or even organizing social activities. Offering a listening ear, a shoulder to lean on, or a helping hand, this support network can play a crucial role in the readjustment period. Building a support team can also involve joining support groups or engaging in community-based programs. These forums provide a chance to connect with others who are going through similar experiences, fostering a sense of connection and understanding. Attending support group meetings or participating in activities organized by community programs can foster a sense of belonging, promote social interactions, and enhance overall well-being. The readjustment process after the holiday season can be a challenging time for individuals dealing with depression and other mental health concerns. By collaborating with mental health professionals and creating a network of support, individuals can enhance their well-being and navigate this period more effectively. Mental health professionals can offer valuable guidance and support, while friends, family, and community-based programs can provide emotional support, companionship, and practical assistance. With these resources in place, individuals can build resilience, find comfort, and begin to focus on their journey towards improved mental health.

XXII. CULTIVATING EMOTIONAL RESILIENCE

Cultivating emotional resilience is a crucial component in managing the challenges that individuals may face when readjusting to their daily routines after the holidays. Emotional resilience refers to the ability to adapt and bounce back from difficult situations, and it plays a significant role in maintaining mental well-being. To cultivate this resilience, several strategies can be employed. Firstly, it is essential to acknowledge and validate one's emotions rather than suppressing or denying them. It is natural to experience feelings of sadness or nostalgia after the holiday season, as it signifies the end of a joyful and celebratory period. By accepting these emotions and giving oneself permission to feel them, individuals can prevent emotional bottling up and its subsequent negative impact on mental health. Developing a support system is vital in fostering emotional resilience. Whether it be friends, family, or professional therapists, having a network of individuals who can provide guidance and empathy can significantly aid in overcoming challenges. They can offer a listening ear, provide different perspectives, and offer emotional support, thereby alleviating feelings of loneliness and isolation that may arise during this readjustment period. Engaging in self-care activities is another strategy that can contribute to emotional resilience. Taking time to engage in activities that bring joy and relaxation can help individuals recharge and counteract the stress and pressure of transitioning back to daily routines. This can involve partaking in hobbies, practicing Mindfulness and meditation, or engaging in physical exercise. Fostering positive thinking patterns can play a crucial role in cultivating emotional resilience. By challenging negative thoughts and reframing them in a more positive and realistic light, individuals can cultivate a sense of hope and optimism as they navigate the challenges of returning to routine. It is important to establish healthy coping mechanisms to manage stress effectively. This can involve developing healthy routines, practicing time-management skills, setting realistic goals, and seeking professional help when needed. By implementing these strategies, individuals can nurture their emotional resilience and equip themselves with the necessary tools to navigate the readjustment period with a sense of strength and resilience. Cultivating emotional resilience is vital in managing the challenges of returning to routine after the holidays. By acknowledging and validating one's emotions, building a support network, engaging in self-care activities, fostering positive thinking patterns, and establishing healthy coping mechanisms, individuals can develop the resiliency necessary to thrive during this readjustment period. Emotional resilience allows individuals to bounce back from adversity, maintain mental well-being, and embrace the opportunities and growth that come from embracing routine.

EMBRACING EMOTIONAL DISCOMFORT

Recognizing that post-holiday emotions are valid and temporary helps individuals develop emotional resilience.

Embracing emotional discomfort is an essential aspect of developing emotional resilience. It is crucial to recognize that post-holiday emotions are completely valid and temporary. After the holidays, individuals often experience a wide range of emotions, including sadness, anxiety, and even a sense of emptiness. These emotions can arise due to a variety of reasons, such as the contrast between the joy and excitement of the festive season and the return to mundane daily routines. Equally, the pressure to create memorable experiences during the holidays can lead to high expectations that may not have been met, resulting in disappointment and a sense of letdown afterwards. For those who have lost loved ones or are separated from family and friends, the holidays can intensify feelings of loneliness and grief. Acknowledging and accepting these post-holiday emotions as valid is the first step towards developing emotional resilience. Many individuals may feel compelled to dismiss or suppress these emotions, considering them unwarranted or inconsequential. Invalidating these feelings can worsen mental well-being in the long run. Recognizing that it is normal to experience emotional discomfort after the holidays allows individuals to navigate these emotions with greater self-compassion and understanding. It enables individuals to recognize that the intensity of these feelings will dissipate over time.

Developing emotional resilience involves not just acknowledging the validity of post-holiday emotions but also understanding that they are temporary. Emotions are fluid and ever-changing, and recognizing their transitory nature can provide individuals with reassurance during challenging times. By reminding themselves that these feelings will ebb and flow, individuals can prevent themselves from becoming stuck in a negative emotional state. Instead of perceiving post-holiday emotions as an indication of personal failure or permanent despair, individuals can view them as a natural part of the human experience that will eventually fade away. Accepting the transience of post-holiday emotions can enhance an individual's capacity to face future challenges. By weathering emotional discomfort and recognizing its temporary nature, individuals become more resilient in dealing with life's ups and downs. This enables them to approach future hurdles with a greater sense of confidence and adaptability. In summary, embracing emotional discomfort and recognizing the validity and transience of post-holiday emotions are crucial for developing emotional resilience. Acknowledging these emotions as normal and temporary allows individuals to navigate them with self-compassion and understanding. By accepting the transience of emotional discomfort, individuals can develop greater resilience and better cope with future challenges. Embracing emotional discomfort helps individuals not only survive but also thrive in the face of adversity.

DEVELOPING COPING SKILLS

Learning and practicing healthy coping skills empowers individuals to manage post-holiday stressors effectively.

Developing coping skills is essential for individuals to effectively manage post-holiday stressors. The holiday season often brings about a myriad of emotions and pressures, and it is common for individuals to feel overwhelmed in the aftermath. By learning and practicing healthy coping skills, individuals can regain empowerment and take control of their mental well-being. Firstly, developing coping skills allows individuals to identify and acknowledge their emotions. Often, people tend to suppress their feelings or deny their impact on their mental state. By actively engaging in coping strategies, individuals can create a space for themselves to reflect on their emotions, understand their triggers, and gradually accept their validity. Secondly, coping skills provide individuals with the tools to handle stress and anxiety triggered by post-holiday pressures. These pressures may include financial strain, the pressure to meet societal expectations, or a sense of letdown after the holiday fervor. Through coping skills such as deep breathing exercises, meditation, or engaging in hobbies, individuals can manage stress levels, find solace, and cultivate a sense of tranquility amidst the chaos. Coping skills enable individuals to establish boundaries and prioritize self-care post-holidays. Often, the holiday season involves excessive socializing, familial obligations, and an overwhelming workload. This can lead individuals to neglect their own needs and wellbeing. By practicing healthy coping skills such as assertive communication and time management, individuals can set clear boundaries, prioritize their own self-care, and prevent burnout. Developing coping skills fosters resilience and adaptability in individuals. Life is full of uncertainties and challenges, and the ability to cope effectively is crucial. By learning coping strategies, individuals gain the resilience needed to bounce back from setbacks, adapt to changing situations, and build a positive attitude towards life. Coping skills encourage individuals to seek social support when needed. There is often a stigma associated with seeking help, as it is seen as a sign of weakness. Coping skills teach individuals that reaching out for support is a sign of strength and self-awareness. Whether it is through professional help, confiding in friends, or participating in support groups, seeking support can significantly alleviate post-holiday stressors. Developing coping skills is paramount in managing the post-holiday stressors effectively. By cultivating these skills, individuals gain insight into their emotions, find strategies to handle stress, establish boundaries, foster resilience, and seek support when needed. Engaging in healthy coping mechanisms empowers individuals to regain control over their mental well-being and navigate the post-holiday period with resilience and confidence.

NURTURING EMOTIONAL WELL-BEING

Prioritizing emotional well-being through self-care, therapy, and self-reflection contributes to overall emotional resilience during the readjustment period. Nurturing emotional well-being is imperative, particularly during the readjustment period after the holidays. This period can trigger feelings of depression and disrupt relationships as individuals struggle to transition back into their regular routines. To combat these challenges, it is necessary to prioritize emotional well-being through methods such as self-care, therapy, and self-reflection. Self-care involves activities that promote one's physical, mental, and emotional health. Engaging in regular exercise, practicing Mindfulness , and ensuring adequate sleep are all examples of self-care techniques that can enhance emotional resilience. By taking care of oneself, individuals are better equipped to manage stressors and emotions that arise during the readjustment period. Therapy is another crucial element in nurturing emotional well-being during this time. Seeking professional help from therapists or counselors can provide individuals with the tools and support they need to navigate through this transition effectively. Therapists can help individuals identify any underlying issues or triggers of depression, as well as offer coping mechanisms and strategies to handle negative emotions. Through therapy, individuals can gain insight into their own thoughts, feelings, and behaviors, ultimately enhancing their emotional resilience. In addition to self-care and therapy, self-reflection plays a vital role in nurturing emotional well-being during the readjustment period. Taking the time to reflect on one's emotions and experiences can lead to a deeper understanding of their emotional states. Journaling, meditation, or engaging in creative outlets are effective ways to engage in self-reflection. By reflecting on their emotions, individuals can identify any patterns or triggers that contribute to their emotional well-being, and subsequently develop effective strategies to manage and regulate these emotions. Prioritizing emotional well-being through self-care, therapy, and self-reflection is essential during the readjustment period. By engaging in self-care techniques, individuals can promote their overall emotional resilience by fostering physical, mental, and emotional well-being. Seeking therapy can provide individuals with the necessary support and guidance to navigate through the challenges of this period. Self-reflection allows individuals to gain insight into their own emotions and experiences, leading to a deeper understanding of themselves and their emotional needs. By actively nurturing emotional well-being during the readjustment period, individuals can enhance their ability to cope with depression, maintain healthy relationships, and successfully transition back into their normal routines. During the holiday season, many individuals experience a heightened sense of joy, togetherness, and excitement. As the holiday season comes to an end, individuals may find it challenging to readjust to their daily routines, leading to feelings of depression and relationship strain. It is not uncommon for individuals to feel a sense of emptiness or sadness once the festivities are over, known as post-holiday depression. This condition can be attributed to various factors, such as the contrast between the joyful holiday atmosphere and the mundane daily grind, the resurfacing of underlying personal issues during periods of reflection, or a general dissatisfaction with one's life. The abrupt transition from the holiday season to regular routines can leave individuals feeling overwhelmed and unfulfilled. The end of the holiday season often marks the return of long-distance relationships and separations that were temporarily put on hold during the festive period. These separations can trigger feelings of anxiety, sadness, and even resentment for those involved. For couples in long-distance relationships, the holiday season may provide a rare opportunity to spend quality time together. Once the festivities end, the reality of being apart for an extended period sets in, contributing to a sense of loneliness and despair. Such feelings can lead to relationship strain, as partners struggle to cope with the distance and readjust to their regular lives without the emotional support they had during the holidays. In addition to post-holiday depression and relationship strain, readjusting to regular routines after a long break can be a challenging process. The absence of structure and responsibilities during the holiday season creates a stark contrast with the demands and expectations of daily life. This abrupt shift can be overwhelming and may leave individuals feeling disoriented and unmotivated. The lack of immediate gratification and excitement that comes with the holiday season can further contribute to a general mood of dissatisfaction and low energy levels. Thus, readjustment after the holidays requires individuals to reestablish a sense of purpose, regain motivation, and find joy in everyday activities.

To overcome the challenges associated with readjustment after the holidays, individuals can adopt various strategies. Seeking support from friends, family, or mental health professionals can provide a valuable outlet for expressing feelings of sadness or frustration. Engaging in self-care activities, such as exercise,

Mindfulness , or creative outlets, can also help manage post-holiday depression. Couples in long-distance relationships may benefit from setting clear communication goals and making plans for future visits to reduce the impact of separation. Individuals can focus on creating a sense of balance and purpose in their daily lives by setting achievable goals, developing new hobbies or interests, and maintaining a positive mindset.

The end of the holiday season can bring about feelings of depression, strain in relationships, and difficulties in readjustment. Understanding the factors contributing to post-holiday depression and relationship strain can help individuals navigate this challenging period. By seeking support, practicing self-care, and establishing a sense of purpose, individuals can successfully transition back to their regular routines and find fulfillment in their everyday lives.

XXIII. MAINTAINING PERSPECTIVE

Maintaining perspective is a crucial aspect of navigating the challenges that arise after the holidays. In the days and weeks following the cheerful festivities, many individuals find themselves grappling with depression, strained relationships, and difficulties readjusting to their regular routines. Depression often creeps in when the contrast between the joyous holiday season and the more mundane reality of everyday life becomes stark. It is essential to remember that feeling down during this time is a common experience and does not imply personal failure. Rather than succumbing to feelings of despair, individuals should strive to take a step back and analyze the situation from a broader perspective. They should remind themselves of the impermanent nature of emotions, knowing that depressive episodes will eventually pass. It is important to recognize the potential triggers of depression and to take proactive steps towards managing them. Engaging in activities that bring pleasure and practicing self-care can significantly contribute to lifting one's mood. Maintaining open lines of communication with trusted loved ones can provide the much-needed support and alleviate feelings of isolation. Relationships, often under strain during the holiday season, also require a conscious effort to maintain perspective. Close quarters, high expectations, and busyness can put a strain on even the strongest bonds. Recognizing that these conflicts are temporary and do not define the overall health of a relationship is essential. Instead of dwelling on arguments or resentments, individuals should strive to focus on the positive aspects of their relationships. Expressing gratitude and engaging in meaningful conversations can help repair any rifts that may have developed during the hectic holiday period. Readjusting to routine can be challenging as the festivities have disrupted our usual schedules and expectations. It is crucial to remember that adapting to change takes time and patience. Instead of feeling overwhelmed, individuals should approach this period as an opportunity for growth and self-improvement. Establishing a structured routine, setting achievable goals, and gradually reintegrating everyday responsibilities can help ease the transition. By maintaining perspective and acknowledging that challenges are part of the natural ebb and flow of life, individuals can reclaim a sense of control and find comfort in the familiar. It is through these mindful efforts that individuals can overcome post-holiday difficulties, emerge stronger and more resilient, and cultivate a healthier outlook on life.

EMBRACING THE POST-HOLIDAY PERIOD

Recognizing the post-holiday period as a time for growth, reflection, and opportunity fosters a positive perspective.

Embracing the post-holiday period is crucial in recognizing it as a time for growth, reflection, and opportunity, ultimately fostering a positive perspective. The holiday season is often associated with joy and merriment, but the end of this period can lead to a sense of melancholy and letdown. Understanding the potential for personal growth during this time can help individuals navigate through the transition with ease. Reflection is an essential aspect of this process, offering the chance to evaluate past experiences and identify areas for improvement. By taking the time to reflect on the holiday season, individuals can gain insight into their own behaviors and emotions, equipping them with knowledge that can aid in personal growth. The post-holiday period provides the opportunity to set new goals and intentions for the upcoming year. Whether it is focusing on personal well-being or professional development, this time allows individuals to establish clear objectives and take deliberate actions towards achieving them. Recognizing the post-holiday period as a time for opportunity can help individuals find meaning and purpose in their everyday lives. Rather than viewing it solely as the end of a festive season, individuals can use this time as a launching pad for new endeavors and endeavors. For instance, one might take up a new hobby, explore different career options, or engage in community service, all of which can enrich personal growth and create a sense of fulfillment. The post-holiday period presents an opportunity for individuals to establish or strengthen their relationships. While the holiday season often revolves around spending time with loved ones, the post-holiday period provides the chance to deepen these connections further. Whether it is planning regular meetups, initiating conversations about future plans, or simply expressing gratitude for the support received during the holidays, relationships can flourish during this time. By embracing the post-holiday period as a time for growth, reflection, and opportunity, individuals can cultivate a positive perspective and navigate the transition back to routine with less difficulty. Instead of dwelling on the end of the holiday season, individuals can focus on the potential for personal development, establish new goals, find meaning in everyday activities, and strengthen relationships. This mindset can lead to a more fulfilled and contented post-holiday period, setting the stage for a successful year ahead.

FOCUSING ON THE BIGGER PICTURE

Understanding that the holiday season is just one aspect of life helps individuals put post-holiday challenges into perspective. The holiday season is often viewed as a time of joy, celebration, and togetherness. Once the festivities have come to an end, many individuals struggle to readjust to their regular routines and face what may seem like insurmountable post-holiday challenges. In order to effectively navigate these challenges, it is essential to focus on the bigger picture and understand that the holiday season is just one aspect of life. By recognizing this, individuals can put their post-holiday struggles into perspective and find solace in the fact that they are not alone in their experiences. Firstly, it is important to acknowledge that the holiday season is a fleeting moment in time. While it may bring joy and happiness, it is not meant to last forever. It is a temporary break from reality, where individuals can indulge in festivities, spend time with loved ones, and escape the pressures of everyday life. Once the holiday season is over, it is crucial to recognize that life goes on and that there will inevitably be challenges to face. By understanding this, individuals can avoid placing too much emphasis on the post-holiday blues and instead focus on finding ways to adapt and cope with the changes that lie ahead. It is essential to remember that everyone experiences post-holiday challenges in some form or another. Whether it be feeling overwhelmed by the return to work or school, struggling with financial burdens after excessive spending, or perhaps even experiencing a sense of loneliness after the festive season, these difficulties are universally felt. Reminding oneself that these challenges are not unique to them can provide comfort and reassurance, making it easier to navigate through this transitional period. Taking a step back and focusing on the broader perspective can help individuals find meaning in their post-holiday struggles. While it may be tempting to dwell on the negative aspects of readjustment, it is also important to remember the positive aspects that come along with it. For example, the post-holiday period provides an opportunity for personal growth and self-reflection. It allows individuals to evaluate their goals and aspirations for the upcoming year, and to create a plan of action to achieve them. By reframing post-holiday challenges as opportunities for growth and self-improvement, individuals can approach them with a more positive mindset, making the transition smoother and more manageable. Understanding that the holiday season is just one aspect of life can help individuals put post-holiday challenges into perspective. By recognizing that the holiday season is temporary, that post-holiday struggles are common, and that these challenges offer opportunities for personal growth, individuals can approach this transitional period with a more positive mindset. The post-holiday blues may feel overwhelming at times, but by focusing on the bigger picture, individuals can find solace and motivation to navigate through these challenges and return to their regular routines more effectively.

EMBRACING CHANGE AND GROWTH

Embracing the changes and growth that occur during the post-holiday period allows individuals to move forward and thrive.

The post-holiday period can often be a time of mixed emotions, as the festive season comes to an end and individuals are forced to readjust to their regular routines. It is during this period that individuals have the opportunity to reflect on the changes that have taken place and embrace the growth that has occurred. The holidays can bring about a renewed sense of purpose and perspective, as people spend time with loved ones and engage in activities that bring them joy. This can lead to a greater understanding of oneself and what truly matters in life. By embracing these changes and growth, individuals can move forward with a renewed sense of purpose and determination. It is important to recognize that change is a natural part of life and resisting it only serves to hinder personal growth. In order to thrive, individuals must be willing to adapt and embrace the new opportunities that come their way. This may involve letting go of old habits or beliefs that no longer serve a purpose, and being open to trying new things. It can be a challenging process, as it requires stepping out of one's comfort zone and facing uncertainties. The post-holiday period offers a unique opportunity for individuals to reset and reevaluate their lives. By taking the time to reflect on the past and set goals for the future, individuals can use this period of change to their advantage. Embracing change and growth also allows individuals to cultivate resilience and develop a growth mindset. This mindset recognizes that setbacks and challenges are opportunities for learning and personal development. By viewing obstacles as steppingstones rather than roadblocks, individuals can approach life with a sense of optimism and determination. Embracing change and growth can also have a positive impact on relationships. As individuals grow and change, so do the dynamics within relationships. It is important to recognize and embrace these changes, rather than trying to resist or control them. By doing so, individuals can foster healthier and more fulfilling relationships. Embracing the changes and growth that occur during the post-holiday period is essential for personal and relational well-being. It allows individuals to move forward with a renewed sense of purpose and determination, and opens the door to new opportunities and experiences. By embracing change and growth, individuals can cultivate resilience, develop a growth mindset, and foster healthier relationships. In doing so, they can thrive in all aspects of their lives. The holiday season is often seen as a time of joy and celebration, filled with family gatherings, festive decorations, and an abundance of good cheer. For many individuals, the post-holiday period can be a challenging time as they try to readjust to their regular routines and cope with the emotional aftermath of the holiday season. One common struggle that individuals may face during this time is depression. The holiday season often brings heightened expectations of happiness and joy, and when these expectations are not met, individuals may find themselves feeling disappointed and let down. This can lead to feelings of sadness, low energy, and a lack of motivation as they try to navigate their way back to their everyday lives. In addition to the emotional challenges, the post-holiday period can also put a strain on relationships. During the holiday season, individuals may have spent an increased amount of time with loved ones, creating a sense of closeness and bonding. Once the holidays are over, individuals may find themselves longing for that sense of connection that they felt during the holiday season. This longing can lead to feelings of loneliness and disconnection as individuals try to readjust to their regular routines and establish a sense of normalcy in their relationships. The post-holiday period can be a time of readjustment as individuals try to get back into the swing of their regular routines. After weeks of holiday parties, festive gatherings, and time off from work or school, it can be difficult to transition back into the responsibilities and demands of everyday life. This readjustment period can be especially challenging for individuals who struggle with time management or who have difficulty coping with change. It can take time to get back into the rhythm of work or school, and individuals may find themselves feeling overwhelmed and stressed as they try to meet deadlines and stay on top of their responsibilities. The post-holiday period can be a difficult time for many individuals as they try to navigate the emotional, relational, and logistical challenges of readjusting to their regular routines. It is important for individuals to recognize and validate their own feelings during this time and to seek support when needed. Whether through therapy, reaching out to loved ones, or practicing self-care, individuals can work towards finding a sense of balance and normalcy as they transition back into their everyday lives.

XXIV. CONCLUSION

This essay has explored the underlying factors contributing to depression, relationship strain, and readjustment difficulties after the holiday season. It is evident that the holiday season can have a significant impact on an individual's mental well-being, especially those already prone to depression. The heightened expectations, financial strain, and increased social obligations can exacerbate depressive symptoms and create a sense of alienation. Relationships can also suffer during this time due to the added pressure and strain that the holidays can bring. Communication breakdowns and unrealistic expectations can lead to conflict and dissatisfaction in relationships. Readjustment after the holiday season can be challenging, as individuals must transition from a period of indulgence and relaxation to the demands of everyday life. This sudden shift can contribute to feelings of disappointment and a sense of loss. It is important to note that these difficulties are not insurmountable. By recognizing and addressing the underlying causes of depression, such as unrealistic expectations and stress, individuals can take proactive steps to manage their mental health. This may involve seeking professional help, establishing a support system, and practicing self-care. Similarly, communication and understanding are key in maintaining healthy relationships during the holiday season. Clear and open communication can help manage expectations and reduce conflict, while empathy and compromise foster understanding and strengthen the bond between individuals. Readjustment is a natural part of life after any significant period of change. By embracing the routine and finding joy in the little things, individuals can ease the transition and cultivate a sense of contentment. It is important to remember that setbacks are a normal part of the recovery process, and seeking support from loved ones or professionals can be instrumental in navigating these challenges. Depression, relationship strain, and readjustment difficulties are common after the holidays. By understanding the underlying causes and implementing strategies to manage them, individuals can take active steps towards their well-being and create a more balanced and fulfilling life. It is crucial to prioritize self-care, maintain open lines of communication, and adopt a resilient mindset. Recovery is a journey that requires patience, understanding, and a commitment to one's own mental health.

RECAP THESIS STATEMENT

The post-holiday period brings about challenges such as depression, relationship strain, and readjustment difficulties.

The post-holiday period can be a challenging time for many individuals as they navigate the transition from the festivities and excitement of the holiday season to the return to their regular routine. This period often brings about various hurdles, such as depression, strain in relationships, and difficulties readjusting to the demands of everyday life. Firstly, depression can be a prevalent issue during this time as individuals may experience a sense of letdown or sadness once the holiday season is over. The joy and enthusiasm that accompanied the celebrations are replaced with feelings of emptiness and a lack of purpose. This transition can trigger depressive symptoms, such as low mood, loss of interest and motivation, and difficulties in concentration. Strained relationships can also emerge as a challenge during the post-holiday period. The high expectations and pressures surrounding the holiday season can put a strain on couples or families, leading to conflicts and discord. The stress and financial burden associated with gift-giving, arranging gatherings, and meeting social obligations can cause tension and lead to disagreements. Returning to work or school after a vacation can be particularly challenging for individuals, especially those who have had a prolonged break. Readjusting to a structured routine, dealing with increased responsibilities, and coping with the stress of work or academics can be overwhelming and may contribute to feelings of anxiety and pressure. The transition from a relaxed and carefree mindset to one that is focused and task-oriented can be difficult, leaving individuals feeling overwhelmed and out of sync. The post-holiday period can bring about several challenges that individuals need to navigate. Depression, relationship strain, and readjustment difficulties are common hurdles that many people face during this time. Recognizing these challenges and taking proactive steps to address them, such as seeking support from loved ones or mental health professionals, can help individuals effectively cope with and overcome the post-holiday blues. It is essential to prioritize self-care, engage in activities that bring joy and fulfillment, and practice healthy coping strategies to ensure a smoother transition into the daily routine. Acknowledging and addressing these challenges can empower individuals to navigate this period with resilience and maintain their well-being in the post-holiday period.

ADDRESS SIGNIFICANCE

Recognizing and addressing these challenges can lead to enhanced emotional well-being and a smoother transition back to regular routines. The significance of recognizing and addressing the challenges that arise after the holiday season is crucial for one's emotional well-being and a smoother transition back to regular routines. The post-holiday period can be a vulnerable time for many individuals as they face the pressures of readjusting to their daily lives after a period of relaxation and enjoyment. A lack of awareness and acknowledgment of these challenges can contribute to the development or exacerbation of depression. It is essential to understand the potential impact that the post-holiday period can have on mental health and take proactive steps to address it. By recognizing the challenges that may arise, individuals can better equip themselves to navigate the emotional rollercoaster that comes with this forlorn period. During the holidays, many people experience a heightened sense of joy and connection with loved ones. When the festivities come to an end, the return to regular routines can feel mundane and isolating. The sudden shift from a time filled with social interactions and excitement to a more solitary and monotonous routine can be disheartening. This abrupt change can lead individuals to experience feelings of sadness, loneliness, and a lack of purpose. By acknowledging the significance of this transition, individuals can take proactive steps to cushion the blow and lessen the impact on their emotional well-being. Recognizing and addressing these challenges is also important for maintaining healthy relationships. The post-holiday period can put a strain on relationships as partners, family members, and friends readjust to their usual responsibilities and demands. The disparity between the time spent together during the holidays and the time spent apart can create feelings of distance and disconnection in relationships. Without acknowledging these challenges, misunderstandings and conflicts may arise, further exacerbating the emotional distress experienced during this period. By recognizing the potential strain on relationships and engaging in open and honest communication, individuals can strengthen their bonds and navigate the transition more smoothly. Addressing these challenges can provide individuals with a sense of empowerment and control over their emotional well-being. By acknowledging that the post-holiday period can be emotionally taxing, individuals can actively seek strategies to enhance their emotional well-being. This may involve engaging in self-care practices, seeking support from loved ones or professionals, and setting realistic expectations for oneself. By taking a proactive approach, individuals can regain a sense of agency and navigate this period with greater ease.

Recognizing and addressing the challenges that arise after the holiday season is crucial for enhanced emotional well-being and a smoother transition back to regular routines. By acknowledging the potential impact on mental health, individuals can take proactive steps to navigate this period and prevent the onset or exacerbation of depression. Recognizing the strain on relationships and engaging in open communication can preserve and strengthen connections with loved ones. By addressing these challenges, individuals can regain a sense of control over their emotional well-being and increase their chances of a successful readjustment post-holidays.

FINAL THOUGHTS

By practicing self-care, seeking support, and implementing healthy coping strategies, individuals can navigate the post-holiday period with resilience and pave the way for a fulfilling year ahead. The post-holiday period can be a challenging time for individuals as they readjust to their routine and cope with the emotional aftermath of the holiday season. By practicing self-care, seeking support, and implementing healthy coping strategies, individuals can navigate this period with resilience and pave the way for a fulfilling year ahead. Self-care is essential during this time as it allows individuals to prioritize their mental, emotional, and physical well-being. Engaging in activities that bring joy and relaxation, such as exercise, spending time in nature, or pursuing hobbies, can have a positive impact on one's mental health. Seeking support is crucial in coping with the post-holiday blues. Talking to trusted friends or family members about one's feelings and experiences can provide a sense of validation and comfort. It can also be helpful to seek professional help through therapy or counseling, as trained professionals can provide guidance and support in navigating through this challenging period. Implementing healthy coping strategies can contribute to emotional resilience. This can include practicing Mindfulness and self-reflection to gain insight into one's emotions and thought patterns. Engaging in stress-reducing activities, such as yoga or meditation, can also help individuals manage their stress levels effectively. Finding healthy outlets for expressing emotions, such as journaling or creating art, can provide individuals with a sense of release and self-expression. By practicing self-care, seeking support, and implementing healthy coping strategies, individuals can not only overcome post-holiday blues but also set the foundation for a fulfilling and successful year ahead. Although the adjustment period may be challenging, it is important to remember that it is temporary and that with time and effort, one can regain a sense of stability and contentment. By taking care of oneself and seeking support when needed, individuals can build resilience and develop the tools to navigate the post-holiday period with grace and determination. This period can be seen as an opportunity for growth and self-reflection, setting the stage for a year filled with personal and emotional fulfillment.

BIBLIOGRAPHY

Michael E. McCullough. 'The Psychology of Gratitude.' Robert A. Emmons, Oxford University Press, 2/26/2004

Sayon Mandal. 'The Power of Positive Thinking.' A Practical Guide to Transforming Your Mindset and Achieving Success, Book Rix, 6/10/2023

Shelley E McAlpine. 'A Taste for Recovery.' A Personal Story of Survival and a Roadmap to Restoring Physical Health, HP Lighthouse Company, 11/22/2015

I. Visco. 'Price Expectations in Rising Inflation.' Elsevier, 6/28/2014

Anneliese A. Singh. 'The Queer and Transgender Resilience Workbook.' Skills for Navigating Sexual Orientation and Gender Expression, New Harbinger Publications, 2/2/2018

Kelsey J. Patel. 'Burning Bright.' Rituals, Reiki, and Self-Care to Heal Burnout, Anxiety, and Stress, Harmony/Rodale, 4/28/2020

Jennifer Fitzgerald. 'An Emotionally Focused Workbook for Couples.' The Two of Us, Veronica Kallos-Lilly, Routledge, 12/20/2021

Alfred Dean. 'Social Support, Life Events, and Depression.' Nan Lin, Academic Press, 10/22/2013

Lori J. Spina. 'Harnessing Change to Develop Talent and Beat the Competition.' James D. Spina, Emerald Group Publishing, 6/3/2020

James Clear. 'Atomic Habits.' An Easy & Proven Way to Build Good Habits & Break Bad Ones, Penguin, 10/16/2018

Riccardo Rebonato. 'Coherent Stress Testing.' A Bayesian Approach to the Analysis of Financial Stress, John Wiley & Sons, 6/10/2010

Steven Kramer. 'The Progress Principle.' Using Small Wins to Ignite Joy, Engagement, and Creativity at Work, Teresa Amabile, Harvard Business Press, 7/19/2011

Karyn I Morgan. 'Psychiatric Mental Health Nursing.' Concepts of Care in Evidence-Based Practice, Mary C Townsend, F.A. Davis, 10/19/2017

Kenneth W. Wanberg. 'Criminal Conduct and Substance Abuse Treatment for Adolescents: Pathways to Self-Discovery and Change.' The Provider's Guide, Harvey B. Milkman, SAGE Publications, 7/23/2012

Billy T. Ogletree. 'Augmentative and Alternative Communication.' Challenges and Solutions, Plural Publishing, Incorporated, 12/14/2020

Hugh Schulze. 'Reducing the Stigma of Mental Illness.' A Report from a Global Association, Norman Sartorius, Cambridge University Press, 5/26/2005

Deborah Serani. 'Living with Depression.' Why Biology and Biography Matter Along the Path to Hope and Healing, Rowman & Littlefield, 9/11/2023

Jennifer L. Hughes. 'CBT for Depression in Children and Adolescents.' A Guide to Relapse Prevention, Betsy D. Kennard, Guilford Publications, 4/5/2016

Michael Tushman. 'Competing by Design.' The Power of Organizational Architecture, David Nadler, Oxford University Press, USA, 7/10/1997

Julie Olsen Edwards. 'Anti-Bias Education for Young Children and Ourselves, Second Edition.' Louise Derman-Sparks, National Association for the Education of Young Children, 1/1/2020

Leland Whitney Crafts. 'Routine and Varying Practice as Preparation for Adjustment to a New Situation.' Columbia university, 1/1/1927

Division of Behavioral and Social Sciences and Education. 'Parenting Matters.' Supporting Parents of Children Ages 0-8, National Academies of Sciences, Engineering, and Medicine, National Academies Press, 11/21/2016

Howard Whitton. 'Managing Conflict of Interest in the Public Sector.' A Toolkit, Organisation for Economic Co-operation and Development, 1/1/2005

Julie Schwartz Gottman. 'Eight Dates.' Essential Conversations for a Lifetime of Love, John Gottman, Workman Publishing, 2/5/2019

Michael Todd. 'Relationship Goals Challenge.' Thirty Days from Good to Great, Crown Publishing Group, 12/29/2020

Margaret Wehrenberg. 'The 10 Best-Ever Depression Management Techniques: Understanding How Your Brain Makes You Depressed and What You Can Do to Change It.' W. W. Norton & Company, 2/14/2011

Truman Capote. 'In Cold Blood.' Random House Publishing Group, 2/19/2013

Ronda Hughes. 'Patient Safety and Quality.' An Evidence-based Handbook for Nurses, Agency for Healthcare Research and Quality, U.S. Department of Health and Human Services, 1/1/2008